The End of Stigma?

KU-574-492

This innovative book investigates the roots of contemporary experiences of stigma, throwing new light on the phenomenon by examining a variety of long-term conditions.

Behaviour, lifestyle and identity are no longer the results of mass production by social class and nation, but increasingly the quirky and unique eccentricities of the individual as consumer, reflexive citizen and free agent. But if the hallmark of the post-modern world is endless variety and unlimited subcultural freedom, should we not be witnessing 'the end of stigma'? The book takes Fukuyama's notion of 'the end of history' and examines contemporary challenges to the stigma associated with chronic illness.

Award-winning author Gill Green examines cases of HIV, mental illness and substance misuse to provide new insights into stigma in health. She demonstrates that people with long-term conditions refuse to be defined by their condition and highlights their increasingly powerful voice. *The End of Stigma?* will be of interest to a wide range of students and health professionals in medical sociology, health studies and social care.

Gill Green is a Professor of Medical Sociology at the University of Essex, UK. Her main research interest is the experiential and social consequences of long-term illness.

WITHDRAWN

LIVERPOOL JMU LIBRARY

3 1111 01264 9677

The End of Stigma?

Changes in the social experience
of long-term illness

Gill Green

Routledge
Taylor & Francis Group

LONDON AND NEW YORK

LIVERPOOL
JOHN MOORES UNIVERSITY
AVRIL ROBARTS LRC
TEL. 0151 231 4022

First published 2009
by Routledge
2 Park Square, Milton Park, Abingdon, Oxon OX14 4RN

Simultaneously published in the USA and Canada
by Routledge
270 Madison Avenue, New York, NY 10016

*Routledge is an imprint of the Taylor & Francis Group, an informa
business*

© 2009 Gill Green

Typeset in Sabon by Prepress Projects Ltd, Perth, UK
Printed and bound in Great Britain by TJ International Ltd, Padstow,
Cornwall

All rights reserved. No part of this book may be reprinted or
reproduced or utilised in any form or by any electronic, mechanical,
or other means, now known or hereafter invented, including
photocopying and recording, or in any information storage or
retrieval system, without permission in writing from the publishers.

British Library Cataloguing in Publication Data
A catalogue record for this book is available from the British Library

Library of Congress Cataloging in Publication Data
Green, Gill, 1956–
The end of stigma?: changes in the social experience of long term
illness/Gill Green.
p.; cm.
1. Chronic diseases – Social aspects. 2. Stigma (Social psychology) I.
Title.
[DNLM: 1. Chronic Disease – psychology. 2. Prejudice. 3.
Stereotyping. WT 30 G796e 2009]
RC108.G75 2009
306.4´61 – dc22
2008036516

ISBN 10: 0–415–37624–6 (hbk)
ISBN 10: 0–415–37625–4 (pbk)
ISBN 10: 0–203–88179–6 (ebk)

ISBN 13: 978–0–415–37624–2 (hbk)
ISBN 13: 978–0–415–37625–9 (pbk)
ISBN 13: 978–0–203–88179–8 (ebk)

Contents

Contents

Preface

My personal journey for this book starts in Glasgow in the 1990s when I was involved in a project about the experiences of people with HIV at a time when HIV was so highly stigmatized that there was pervasive and shocked media coverage when Princess Diana touched a person who was known to be HIV positive.

At about this time I saw the show *Freaks* by Compagnie Genevieve de Kermabon at the Tramway theatre, which told the story of the performers in a 'freak show'. The cast were mainly disabled people, many of whom had severe impairments, yet they performed a range of extraordinary physical feats such as a man without legs 'walking' on his hands along a tightrope. What I was seeing was disabled stigmatized 'freaks' performing incredible tricks and in so doing challenging the stigmatized view of them.

When I watched *Freaks* I was witnessing the powerful two-way interaction described by Goffman as a defining feature of stigma. According to Goffman (1963), stigma is a social product generated by social interactions in which potentially stigmatizing attributes (in this case those associated with disabled bodies) are deemed as different or inferior. *Freaks* challenged this stigmatizing process. The audience was clearly impressed by the feats on display and the different disabled bodies of the cast became objects of open admiration that cannot fail to have enhanced the identity of the cast, promoted their self-worth and most certainly affirmed that they were not the *Freaks* of the show's title. In a classic post-modern twist, perhaps that was the audience.

Since this time I have conducted research with people living with a range of long-term conditions, resulting in a number of articles and a book. My thinking on the topic, however, acquired strong personal relevance when I was diagnosed with multiple sclerosis (MS) in 1999, having had numb legs, which made me walk haltingly for a few weeks. I made a full recovery and was without further symptoms for nine years. Could the diagnosis have been wrong? It seems not. Whilst I was writing this book the vision in my right eye became blurred and distorted, which was disorienting as the world looked disjointed. Several weeks later my sight returned to normal. However, I was given a diagnosis of optic neuritis (inflammation of the optic nerve), a classic symptom of MS, so all hopes were dashed that maybe the neurologist got the diagnosis wrong nine years ago. In this sense I am now one of the inhabitants of what Susan Sontag calls the 'kingdom of the sick', as I am someone who lives with a long-term condition.

Whom to tell? Family and friends of course – I need their support. But what about the wider net? What about work? If illness-related stigma is no longer an issue, why don't I tell everyone I come into contact with?

In the future I may have no choice as the disabling impact that MS may have on my body may be visible and profound, but this is not the case today. I am well and function 'normally'.

But I choose not to tell everyone. Why not?

- There is no need to tell everyone. MS is not affecting my functioning or my interactions with those I come into contact with so they don't need to know. There are many details of my personal life that I choose not to share with the majority of people I come into contact with and this is one of them.
- I don't want people to define me as sick when I am currently healthy. I hope to go on being healthy and I may be one of the 'lucky ones' with MS whose life is not severely disrupted through illness. Hopefully relapses will be infrequent and recovery from them will be good and I may be able to live a relatively MS-free life despite having an MS diagnosis. In this scenario there may never be a need for people to know I have MS.
- I may be labelled a fraud. In the nine symptom-free years following diagnosis, a couple of friends asked, 'have you really got MS?', as I didn't seem like someone with MS, a disease associated with progressively debilitating disability. I even began to doubt it myself.
- I don't want people to define me as 'the person with MS'. I am concerned that people will equate the diagnosis with personal tragedy and lost opportunities, if not now then in the future. It is something I myself worry about from time to time. I have written academic papers about the restricted opportunities associated with MS. The evidence is there. But I don't want the possibility or even probability of ill health and disability in the future to define the public persona of who I am in the present.
- I am concerned that some people may label me as a 'poor bet' for the future, particularly in the workplace. I may be less likely to gain promotion in my current place of work and less likely to be appointed to a new job. Who would choose to employ someone who has an increased risk of becoming ill and disabled?

These are the reasons why I choose not to 'wear' my diagnosis publicly. They are essentially related to presentation of self and my perception of a mismatch between how others view MS and how well this fits with the image of self I project. I think others categorize people with MS as 'ill' yet I currently see myself as someone who is 'well'.

Fear of stigmatizing responses has played only a minor role in my decisions about disclosure of my diagnosis and my experience thus far is that any fears I have about being treated differently by people or disadvantaged in the workplace as a result of having an MS diagnosis have never materialized. Friends, colleagues and managers I have disclosed my diagnosis to are wholly supportive and, taking their lead from me, appear to have put thoughts about MS firmly on a back burner.

Am I therefore affected by the stigma of MS? In general, I would say 'no'. Even though I think about disclosure from time to time and reflect upon public attitudes to people with MS, I do not feel stigmatized by the diagnosis. To what extent is this related to dimensions of the technological, personal and organizational challenges that feature in this book?

I have not had any support from technology, other than an inconclusive MRI scan, and my diagnosis was based on presenting symptoms. There is little hope for a cure for MS, almost certainly not in my lifetime, and even the most sophisticated disease-modifying treatments only slow down progression by about a third. My condition has not yet reached a stage in which these expensive drugs are recommended or paid for according to the guidelines produced by the National Institute for Health and Clinical Excellence. Yet technology will certainly play a part as relapses and any residual disability resulting from them progress. There is a huge range of therapeutic treatments to lessen the impact of symptoms, ranging from physiotherapy to cannabis and any number of disability aids.

To date, the personal challenge has had more relevance and has provided a clear goal to aim for – to still be me. A long-term diagnosis, even if one has no or minimal symptoms, still has an impact upon one's sense of self. As illness progresses, and particularly if and when it becomes disabling and former pursuits have to be abandoned, the assault on the self becomes more profound. The self will of course be affected, modified and changed by illness but it does not have to be swamped by it. The fight to retain one's sense of self and not be wholly defined by one's illness is evident at all stages of long-term illness.

The organizational challenge has also offered support. Shortly after diagnosis, I attended a 'Getting to grips with MS' course put on by my local branch of the national MS Society. It was organized by people with MS for people recently diagnosed with MS. The six sessions covered all sorts of MS-related topics and advice about living with MS, such as exercise; support from the neuro-rehabilitation unit; current knowledge and research on MS; disability-related grants and welfare payments. It was also an opportunity to get to know and share concerns with others on the course. Thereafter I have remained in touch with the MS Society, albeit at a distance; I find the monthly newsletter helpful and informative and I regularly look for information on their website. I took part in their successful campaign to obtain more widespread provision of disease-modifying drugs by writing to my Member of Parliament. I applied for and obtained an MS Society grant for research into the social and economic impact of MS. I am pleased that the MS Society is there.

So, from a personal perspective, I would say that the challenges to stigma identified in this book have helped me to come to terms with my diagnosis and not to feel stigmatized by it. My experience of long-term illness is thus far fairly limited with only very short periods of actively 'being ill', and therefore offers only a limited insight into the personal world of long-term conditions and stigma. I am not a classic exemplar to illustrate the main arguments put forward in this book. Nor is this book about my own experience of illness. However, personal experience of having a long-term condition has altered my perspective. It therefore seems important at the outset to identify myself as a person with MS.

I would like to acknowledge the help, assistance and support of a number of individuals and institutions without whom this book would not have been written.

The empirical research reported on here was funded from a number of sources: the HIV research was funded by the Medical Research Council of Great Britain and carried out when I worked at the MRC Medical Sociology Unit, Glasgow University, and I also draw upon a scoping exercise I conducted that was funded by the British HIV Association (2003); both the research about people with drug and alcohol problems and that about mental health service users were funded by the National Health Service (2000–3); the research about people with MS was funded by the MS Society (2003–4).

Although this book puts forth an original argument, portions of data presented here have been included in previously published work, which has been drawn upon or quoted from to support the present analysis. The publishers of these works have kindly granted permission to reproduce or otherwise draw upon selected extracts for this book. They are: Taylor & Francis (from the book *The Endangered Self* and journals *Deviant Behavior* and *Journal of Mental Health*) and Elsevier Publications (*Social Science & Medicine*).

Thanks also to my longest-standing friend, Hilary Davison, for her permission to use the poems of her late husband Paul Laking, and for her keen interest in my progress with this book.

Over the years I have collaborated with a number of colleagues on research projects about long-term conditions and working with them has undeniably helped to shape my thoughts about stigma and illness. In particular, I would like to thank the following for their input: Hannah Bradby, Louise Marsland, Dan O'Neill, Ewen Speed and the following co-authors of the previously published works cited in this book: Catherine Hayes, Rose Smith, Elisa Sobo, Nigel South and especially Jennie Todd, who in addition kindly provided feedback on an earlier draft of this book.

My major debt is to Charlie Davison, who provided the impetus and invaluable assistance in discussions extending over several months in helping to develop the framework presented in this book. He also provided critical feedback on earlier drafts as well as unwavering support and belief that this book would get written. Without his support, this book would probably not have been started and definitely not completed.

This book is dedicated to the memory of my parents Colette and Michael Green, who taught me to value difference, and to my children, Max, Keith and Stella, in the hope that this value will be passed down through the generations.

1 Challenging stigma

The changing landscape of stigma associated with long-term conditions

> I am a sculptor, living with cancer. Note that I do not say 'I am a cancer patient'. I am *living*, and I just happen to have some cancer.

The above quotation is from the website of a sculptor, John Shonle, and serves as a useful introduction to this book in that it attests to the increased willingness of people living with long-term conditions to acknowledge and talk privately and publicly about their illness but not have their identity defined by it. They are becoming more vocal about their experiences and their needs whilst at the same time resisting, increasingly actively, the stigma and moral weakness traditionally associated with illness. We are witnessing a realignment of social relationships – the old order in which the sick and disabled are disempowered and marginalized is being replaced by a world characterized by their increasing confidence and a reassertion of their essential personhood. In contrast to the traditional notion of a long-term condition defining a person and their identity, people living with long-term conditions are increasingly resisting such labels and are actively defining their illness in relation to who they are.

These processes of redefinition can be seen as aspects of a wider and more profound set of socio-cultural changes, identified by sociologists as the move to the late modern or post-modern era. Since the early development of industrial societies, behaviour, lifestyle and identity have been the products of the relations of production and overarching political systems, articulated through an individual's membership of mass agglomerations such as social class and nation. The late twentieth century, however, witnessed the fracturing of traditional economic relations, the breakup of the big post-war political blocs and the burgeoning of electronic means of communication. These structural changes have brought us into an era in which behaviour, lifestyle and identity are increasingly determined by the individual as consumer and the quirky, unique and often playful eccentricities of the reflexive citizen as free agent.

LIVERPOOL JOHN MOORES UNIVERSITY
LEARNING & INFORMATION SERVICES

In the political and economic arena, this process was characterized by Fukuyama (Fukuyama, 1989; Fukuyama, 1992) as 'the end of history', as there is no longer the cultural space for the large-scale ideological battles of the pre-modern age:

> What we may be witnessing is not just the end of the Cold War, or the passing of a particular period of post-war history, but the end of history as such: that is, the end point of mankind's ideological evolution and the universalization of Western liberal democracy as the final form of human government.
>
> (Fukuyama, 1989: 4)

'The end of history' describes the late twentieth-century ascendancy of western liberal democracy and the 'unabashed victory of economic and political liberalism' (Fukuyama, 1989: 3). Building upon Hegel's concept of the end of history following Napoleon's victory against the Prussians at the battle of Jena in 1806 and the triumph of the ideas of *liberté, égalité* and *fraternité* of the French revolution, Fukuyama contends that the two major challenges to liberalism in the twentieth century, fascism and communism, are essentially 'dead' as living ideological forces. The former was routed by military defeat and the latter with the tumbling of the Berlin Wall in 1989 and the incipient liberalization of the Chinese economy. He cites as evidence the rapid advancement of liberal economies and consumer culture that seem to promote and preserve liberalism in the political sphere. In contrast the highly centralized socialist-organized economies appear to be 'woefully inadequate in creating what have been termed complex "post-industrial" economies in which information and technological innovation play a much larger role' (Fukuyama, 1992: xv).

The notion of the end of history does not mean that all events and international conflict will cease, as 'history' still has a long way to go in less developed areas of the world and ethnic and nationalist conflicts persist, but rather alludes to the fact that large-scale conflict between big states is passing and this process is linked to the rise of modern political and economic liberalism that appears to be an inevitable 'end-point'.

This book borrows the idea of 'the end of history' and the concept that there is no longer the cultural space for the large-scale ideological battles associated with modernity. I then apply the general notion to the social and cultural experiences of, and responses to, those with long-term conditions in the twenty-first century.

The fracturing of modernist structures, the freeing of social life from traditions and customs, the reflexive (re)structuring of the self, the empowerment of previously disenfranchised groups, and the inexorable rise of identity politics are all features of post-modernity. From a theoretical standpoint such changes will impact on aspects of social relations and self-identity and thus on stigma. Moves to combat the stigma of long-term conditions are apparent in the increasing strength of the user movement, in the Disability Discrimination Act and in the current government modernization agenda. In the light of this post-modern analysis identifying a fragmentation and fracturing of social relations and the emergence of the multifaceted identity, one might expect a reduction in the stigma associated with long-term conditions. If the hallmark of the post-modern world is endless variety and unlimited sub-cultural freedom, should we not be witnessing 'the end of stigma'?

This book asks whether such changes are indeed taking place. It examines contemporary challenges to the stigma associated with long-term conditions and asks whether there has been a perceptible shift in the relationship between long-term conditions and stigma.

Stigma generally denotes the possession of a trait that marks one out as different from others and is negatively regarded. The field is still largely dominated by the work of Goffman, who shows how the 'spoiling process' associated with stigma may eclipse a person's social identity so that s/he is treated as belonging to a stigmatized category (e.g. as 'a nutter', 'a cripple') rather than as an individual, and devalued in the process. There is a wealth of literature about the stigma associated with long-term conditions, in which these processes are described.

Stigma is often portrayed as an inevitable companion of long-term conditions and there is an assumption, supported by a large body of empirical research, that long-term conditions are always accompanied by stigma. The rationale is that society has stigmatizing attitudes towards the chronically ill and they in turn internalize social attitudes towards them, leading to low self-esteem. A number of studies report that stigma associated with long-term illness is more difficult for the ill person to cope with than the physical impact of the illness. This has been reported in respect of people with HIV and other conditions too (Green and Sobo, 2000).

However, this book argues that social attitudes to long-term conditions are changing and as a result asks whether in contemporary society having a diagnosis of a long-term condition automatically leads to stigma. Is it now possible to be ill without stigma? Is it now possible to be ill and actively fight stigmatizing social attitudes rather than internalize them?

A feature of stigma is that it is a culturally relative construction and what is stigmatizing in one place and time may not be so in another. I therefore focus upon recent social changes to see how these have impacted upon the stigma related to long-term conditions and address the question: 'Are we witnessing the end of stigma?' In doing this, I draw upon the testimonies of people living with HIV, people with drug and alcohol problems, and mental health service users. These people's experiences of living with long-term conditions provide a key to understanding the roots of the contemporary experience of stigma. Their stories lead us to ask: 'To what extent are stigma and social exclusion still salient features in the lives of people living with long-term conditions?'

Challenges to the stigmatizing processes around illness and disability have become a feature of popular culture. Newspaper columns, books and 'blogs' written by people with a variety of illnesses have become commonplace in publications and internet sites. Notable milestones along this road have included Oscar Moore's weekly column 'Life as a Person with AIDS' (see also Moore, 1996), John Diamond's newspaper diary and memoir *C: Because Cowards Get Cancer Too* (Diamond, 1998) and Adrian Sudbury's 'Baldy's Blog' about living with leukaemia (Sudbury, 2008). These writings invite the reader to understand and empathize with the dramatic highs and lows, as well as the everyday mundane realities, of the illness experience.

Illness features in soap operas and popular drama such as *The West Wing*, in which the audience follow the (political and illness) 'career' of the President of the United States when he is diagnosed with multiple sclerosis. The rise in documentaries focusing upon a plethora of common as well as hitherto unknown (and increasingly bizarre) conditions attest to the increasing interest in the 'illness experience'. And there are examples of people using their illness to enhance their identity and popularity, a prime example being Pete Bennett, a young man with Tourette's syndrome, who in 2006 was the clear and popular winner of the UK reality show *Big Brother*. The image of him emerging victorious from the 'Big Brother' house is in clear contrast to the sense of shame felt by people with Tourette's syndrome described in the literature (see for example Davis, Davis and Dowler, 2004).

A further challenge to stigma is offered through the advance of technology. This is most clearly shown in the field of disability, in which the advance of new technology can for example stimulate damaged muscles to move. A particularly striking example of technological advance are the carbon-fibre prosthetic limbs (or 'cheetah legs') belonging to the athlete Oscar Pistorius, a double amputee, that enabled him to compete against able-bodied athletes and win a silver medal in the 2007 South African national athletics championships. Such feats challenge former boundaries between abled and disabled bodies.

The key message of such images is to challenge stigma by asserting that people living with long-term conditions are people with a right to full participation in society. Those who traditionally have been defined as 'not normal' or 'other' are challenging the definition of what is 'normal'. This challenge is most apparent among those who perform extraordinary feats or those who have their 15 minutes of fame, and perhaps it symbolizes little more than the fact that there are some social contexts in which a normally stigmatizing attribute becomes affirmative rather than discrediting. But the fact that this is now commonplace, and examples abound of positive images of illness and disability, provokes the question whether this represents a fundamental shift in social relations between the 'normal' and the stigmatized.

Traditional images of stigma associated with long-term conditions

In 1966 a book was published titled *Stigma: The Experience of Disability* (Hunt, 1966a) that was based upon 11 essays written by people with a range of long-term conditions such as muscular dystrophy or rheumatoid arthritis and disabilities either inherent at birth or acquired through illness.

The writers highlight different aspects of the illness experience but all make reference to the negative societal reaction towards their disability or illness condition and concomitant social exclusion. They write about being ostracized from mainstream society and living in an underprivileged, inferior 'sub-world'. Louis Battye, who was disabled from birth, writes, 'We [disabled people] are not full members of that [able bodied] world, and the vast majority of us can never hope to be' (Battye, 1966: 8–9), and Audrey Shepherd, who was left with a disability following polio, refers to treatment of disabled people as 'pursuing a policy of apartheid' (Shepherd, 1966: 64). Margaret Gill, who had polio, talks of the 'shame of disablement and the knowledge of "being different"' (Gill, 1966: 100), a difference that according to Roger Glanville (1966: 73) 'makes one feel not quite right, a little ill at ease, and therefore tense' or, put more succinctly, 'If you are disabled, you don't fit' (ibid.: 78).

A central theme of this edited collection is that disability creates problems not only due to impaired function but also due to 'our relationship with normal people' (Hunt, 1966b: 146). Hunt notes that the sick and disabled challenge ordinary society in the following ways:

- Being unfortunate as a result of lack of opportunities for marriage, children, work, independence, which are seen as key values in society. Disablement is therefore viewed as tragic.
- Being useless on account of the general perception that disabled people are unable to work and make a contribution to society.
- Being different.
- Being oppressed with limited opportunities to take part in ordinary society.
- Being sick and suffering, diseased and in pain.

All the authors writing in this book had physical and not mental impairments but their essays illustrated the way that they were treated not only as physically damaged but also, by extension, as mentally incapacitated. According to Reginald Ford, who had muscular dystrophy, 'To many people still a disabled person *is* a cripple, in the old pitying, derogatory sense, not only in body but also in mind' (Ford, 1966: 31) and as evidence the title of his essay is 'He's a cripple but he's quite intelligent', which is how he had been introduced by an acquaintance to a third party. This theme is echoed and developed by Paul Hunt's observation that 'An almost automatic linkage is made not only between a sick body and a sick mind, but also undoubtedly between an evil body and an evil mind, a warped personality' (Hunt, 1966b: 156). Physical impairment thus leads to a perception among 'normal' people of difference and lack of fit, casting the disabled person as one unable to take part, mentally challenged and altogether unworthy. This trajectory was deemed the 'personal tragedy' perspective by disability theorists at a later date.

Whereas the social stigma of long-term illness and disability is present in all the narratives, a number of the authors also call for action to address the social consequences and limited opportunities engendered by the societal reaction to their condition. This book was later identified as a clarion call for the political activism that was emerging at this time from the disability movement (Thomas, 2007).

One can indeed discern the seeds of many of the battles that people with long-term conditions have later fought: challenging the stereotypes, working for more state support, struggling for greater independence and integration. For example, Denis Creegan asserts his essential personhood when he writes that 'Society has to realize actively that first and foremost we are *people* equally with the non-disabled. Our social needs and aspirations are identical to theirs' (Creegan, 1966: 112). Others call for legislative and policy change, such as more welfare support to address the poverty associated with illness and disability (Brown, 1966).

Paul Hunt (1966b: 157) urges society to listen to the voices of the ill and disabled, saying:

> We are challenging society to take account of us, to listen to what we have to say, to acknowledge us as an integral part of society itself. We do not want ourselves, or anyone else, treated as second class citizens, and put away out of sight and mind.

Hunt went on to become a founder of the Union of the Physically Impaired Against Segregation (UPIAS), which became a key conduit for disabled people's activism against exclusion.

However, none of the writers hold out much hope for major structural change to improve the position of the sick and disabled. Although Paul Hunt calls for resistance to discrimination and prejudice, he also notes in a footnote that 'The elimination of prejudice is not really possible: a helpful social climate can only do so much, and each individual and generation has to renew a fight that cannot be won' (Hunt, 1966b: 154). Reginald Ford, whilst recognizing that easier access to driving and the development of more sophisticated mobility aids will alleviate social ostracism, also notes ruefully that a crutch is still a crutch and 'No mechanical aid is better than the natural member for which it is a substitute' (Ford, 1966: 34).

These essays introduce the key issues arising from stigmatization from the perspective of people with long-term conditions. These ideas have been developed, reformulated, (re)classified and theorized in more recent testimonies of people with long-term conditions and a myriad of empirical and theoretical academic studies, which will be discussed in the following chapters. However, what is of interest is the durability of the issues identified in these essays written over 40 years ago. What has changed dramatically, however, is the social and cultural environment. The seeds of the political user movement have developed apace and flowered to promote greater social inclusion. The sick and disabled are now encouraged and supported by anti-discrimination legislation to find and retain employment. There is active resistance to stigmatization whereby treating the long-term ill as 'victims' of 'personal tragedy' is actively contested. Technological advances lead to disability aids and treatment regimens that enhance opportunities for social participation and inclusion. Had the writers in the 1960s been aware of the speed with which the political movement would develop or the pace of technological advance would they have taken such a pessimistic view in the longer term? What, one wonders, would Reginald Ford, who lamented that 'No mechanical aid is better than the natural member', think of the recent feats of Oscar Postorius and the emerging possibility that prosthetic limbs on the running track may indeed out-perform 'natural legs' for which they are a substitute? The last 40 years have witnessed the development of a number of challenges to the stigma associated with long-term conditions, which are explored in the pages that follow.

Naming and defining: long-term illness, chronic illness or long-term conditions?

Terminology is not neutral and distinctions between, and naming of, illness, handicap, impairment and disability have been hotly contested in the dynamic political environment of disabled activism of the last 25 years (Barnes and Mercer, 2003). Among the emergent radicalism of minority groups seeking 'more control over their lives, the issue of naming – what they are called – was one of the first battlegrounds' (Zola 1993: 167).

This has resulted in a lack of consistency in the definition of disability (Gronvik, 2007). A central inconsistency stems from the fact that the terminology of illness and disability is built upon a biomedical vocabulary, which sits uneasily with those who focus upon the social model. Medical models base their definition of illness and disability upon pathology and the disease diagnosis whereas the social model is based on the extent to which impairment limits opportunities to participate in society because of social barriers (Altman, 2001).

A further issue is that people with long-term conditions struggle to find names and slogans that project a positive image. As Zola (1993) notes, the ill and disabled cannot readily adapt slogans such as 'Black is beautiful' or 'Sisterhood is powerful' as a rallying cry. 'Long live cancer', for example, is not a slogan that people would identify with. Marks (1999: 145) identifies two strategies that have been employed to resist offensive terminology: 'positive naming' and 'defiant self-naming'. The former, such as the change of name of the UK Spastics Society to 'Scope', tends to focus upon 'capacities rather than limitations, and differences rather than deviance' (ibid.: 146). The latter involves use of slogans such as 'Glad to be mad', which reaffirm the illness status, reappropriate derogatory language and thereby challenge the stigmatizing stereotype associated with it.

Additionally there is ongoing debate about the place of the long-term ill within disabled politics. The majority of disabled people in the population are older people with long-term illnesses (Bury, 1997) but, although there is much overlap between long-term illness and disability, the two are not synonymous. In Zola's study of Het Dorp, a bespoke village in the Netherlands for disabled people, he quotes the following exchange he had with a resident about how the village had changed over time:

> 'Well, the big difference is that there are now more diseased people than handicapped.'
> 'I don't understand.'
> 'I mean there are now more people with multiple sclerosis and muscular dystrophy than those who are paraplegics or had polio or some injury. And it's not good.'
> 'Why does this matter?'
> Almost as if to close the discussion, she replied, 'To be handicapped is to be stabilized, to be diseased is *not*.'
>
> (Zola, 1982: 53)

Long-term illness may result in temporary or permanent disability but does not always do so and the illness is often progressive. In contrast a disabled person may not have an illness and the disability does not necessarily change or deteriorate over time. The inter-relationship between chronic illness and disability is encompassed by the modern terminology 'long-term condition', a term that is both less stigmatizing and inclusive of all long-term conditions whatever their origin and prognosis.[1]

The main focus in this book is illness rather than disability, and the empirical research studies that are discussed in Chapters 4, 5 and 6 relate to people with long-term conditions, some of whom have no discernible disability. However, no discussion of stigma can ignore the contribution of the disability movement that has spearheaded the theoretical concept of the social model of disability and been key to the rise of identity politics. Therefore widespread reference is made to the disability literature and the term 'long-term condition' is the principal term used in this book except when referring to a specific illness state or where reference is made to literature that uses the term 'chronic illness'.

What are the challenges?

The cultural change that is taking place can largely be summarized by the word 'empowerment'. The empowerment of those with long-term conditions has its intellectual roots in the emergent Disability Studies literature, which introduced the concept of the social model of disability. This model shifts the problem away from people with disabilities and focuses upon society and social attitudes that create a physical and social environment that socially excludes and oppresses disabled people. The growing and increasingly powerful voice of the user movement both emanated from and helped to strengthen this view by mounting a number of organizational challenges.

The thrust of the argument developed in this book is that in the current culture of the UK we are witnessing a marked decline in (perhaps the forerunner of the end of?) the stigma associated with long-term conditions. The challenges are diverse in nature and origin, ranging from the political, social and cultural to the advance of scientific research. They can be broadly grouped under three headings: organizational, personal and technological.

Organizational challenges

Empowerment of those with long-term conditions is strongly associated with the formation of 'identity politics' (Anspach, 1979). Linked to this movement, user organizations, such as self-help groups that had formerly been primarily therapeutic in aim, became overtly political. The politicization of user movements was greatly accelerated by the radicalism of people with HIV/AIDS who orchestrated a vast array of political action, from demonstrations to health promotion campaigns, to highlight their needs, to lobby for increased resources and to combat the negative societal image associated with what was then a new and frightening disease.

There are now few conditions that are not represented by a user movement and these organizations play an increasingly important role in the development of treatment services and research. There are now few service providers in the UK who do not have some form of user representation among their decision-making bodies. Greater empowerment has also had an impact on legislation, most notably in the UK with the introduction of the Disability Discrimination Act in 1995. In addition, numerous campaigns have aimed to promote the rights of the people with long-term conditions and combat negative societal attitudes.

Personal challenges

Empowerment of service users not only finds expression in political action but also operates at a personal level. Those with long-term conditions increasingly assert their essential personhood and refuse to be defined by their condition. The process of reflexive identity formation, identified by Giddens (1991) as a hallmark of high modernity, has led to many questioning the stigma associated with their condition. Rather than internalizing that stigma to create a negative self-image, there is an increasing willingness to challenge the stigmatizing view and resist the label of moral defectiveness traditionally associated with illness and disability.

Technological challenges

Although the main focus is on social and cultural challenges, the impact of new health technology also needs to be considered as it has particular relevance for illness and disability. Furthermore, cultural change and technological development do not operate in a social vacuum and are in themselves inextricably interlinked. Technological advances mean that there is a profound change in the experience of a number of long-term conditions. HIV, which was previously terminal, is now, although still incurable, relatively well controlled by antiretroviral therapies, at least among HIV-positive people who have access to them. Treatments, such as chemotherapy, which previously created side effects of sufficient severity to require hospitalization or home confinement, now often include drugs that reduce the side effects to such an extent that those undergoing treatment can continue with many aspects of their daily lives.

In addition technological developments make it increasingly possible to 'mask' illness and/or the side effects of treatment. Sophisticated prosthetic body parts make the absence of breasts and limbs less noticeable. Cosmetic surgery can hide innumerable blemishes and illness-related scars.

Scope and organization of the book

This book examines the impact of social and cultural changes described above upon people with a range of long-term conditions, drawing upon current literature as well as primary research that I have conducted with HIV-positive people, people with drug and alcohol problems, and mental health service users. All these conditions are associated with stigma, especially as there is evidence that there is greater stigma attached to conditions for which people are considered culpable (i.e. 'achieved' as a result of behaviour rather than 'ascribed' through genetic make-up, accident or environment), and to those that affect the mind rather than the body (Albrecht, Walker and Levy, 1982).

These empirical studies were conducted over a 15-year period and each one was initially conceived and carried out as a stand-alone study. Each project used a different methodology so the studies are in no sense comparable and no attempt is made to compare different long-term conditions although it is acknowledged that each condition has a somewhat different type of stigma to contend with.

In addition, the main thrust of each of the empirical studies was varied and not necessarily focused primarily upon the stigma associated with the experience of each condition. However, each study generated data that can be used to address the central question of the book and that are combined with evidence from the wider literature to contribute to our understanding of the changing nature of stigma in the twenty-first century.

The groups studied, the stigma associated with each condition and the challenge that is addressed are detailed in Table 1.1. It is important to stress, however, that each illness is associated with a variety of challenges to stigma. For example HIV is chosen as an exemplar of the technological challenge but HIV-positive people are also active in terms of personal and organizational challenges to stigma.

In this introductory chapter, I have begun to unpack the question that forms the title of the book by drawing upon contemporary images of people with long-term conditions and comparing these with traditional images from the past. Contemporary images of people with long-term conditions tend to be more positive than in the past and increasingly challenge stigma by asserting that people with long-term conditions have the right to full participation in society. The major challenges to explore are described and include technological, personal and organizational challenges.

Although Chapters 2 and 3 review the literature, and define the parameters of what follows in the illness-specific chapters, the discussion of previous research is not limited to these early chapters. Throughout the book, I cycle back and forth between empirical data from my own and other studies and the literature and draw upon examples from popular culture and the media where relevant.

Chapter 2 starts with a review of the key features of stigma from both the sociological and psychosocial perspectives, and reviews the literature about the stigma associated with long-term conditions. Much of this literature views long-term illness within an individualized deviance paradigm, which has been challenged by disability theorists who view illness and disability primarily from a perspective of societal oppression. The distinction between stigma and discrimination is discussed in the light of these differing perspectives. So too is the nature of 'power', which underpins both the production of stigma and the associated discrimination and social exclusion.

Chapter 3 considers the technological, personal and organizational challenges to stigma. It examines the fracturing of social relationships in which

Table 1.1 Characteristics of conditions studied

Group	Stigma type	Challenge
HIV-positive people	Blame/deviance/danger	Technological
Substance-using offenders	Blame/deviance/danger	Personal
Mental health service users	Difference/danger	Organizational

the sick and disabled have traditionally been disempowered and the growing ability of people with long-term conditions to publicly claim formerly discredited identities. The technological challenge is discussed with reference to the flexible bodies and fluid identities associated with post-modernism, whereby technology can assist people with long-term conditions to project a positive image and mask formerly visible discrediting features. New mechanisms of self-identity linked to reflexivity are examined to illustrate the shift from 'loss of self', associated with traditional images of illness, to reconstructed empowered identities, which form the core of the personal challenge. The discussion then moves from the personal to the political, charting the rise of identity politics around which the user movement has grown and the organizational challenge has coalesced. This has ensured that the voices of people with long-term conditions have become a dominant force in policy and research agendas, a transformation conceptualized as people with long-term conditions being considered first and foremost as citizens with rights.

Chapters 4, 5 and 6 focus on the specific challenges, and particular conditions are selected as exemplars. Chapter 4 explores the impact of the technological challenge in the form of new drug therapies that control the progression of HIV, a condition that in many ways represented the quintessential stigma experience of the twentieth century, having all the key ingredients associated with high levels of stigmatization. The nature and impact of the stigmatization processes are described using research conducted in the 1990s. This chapter then examines the impact of highly active antiretroviral therapies upon HIV-positive people. It illustrates how technological advances help HIV-positive people to control and conceal their symptoms.

Chapter 5 focuses on the Foucauldian 'dangerous individual' and illustrates how one of the most reviled and stigmatized groups in society reclaims a moral space. To this end narratives of substance-misusing offenders, many of whom have significant mental health problems, are analysed. The analysis seeks to examine how a sense of self is retained in the light of bearing a damning societal label and charts the narrative construction of the self as moral and responsible in response to this label. Substance misusers are thus exemplars of the personal challenge to stigma in that they demonstrate empowerment via assertion of their essential moral personhood.

Chapter 6 explores the organizational challenge to stigma by drawing upon the experiences of mental health service users. Sources of stigma associated with mental illness are explored and the impact of this upon social and economic participation and upon sense of selfhood is discussed with reference to accounts from service users. Active resistance to stigmatizing labels and processes are examined, as is the impact of this challenge upon the position of service users, specifically upon their citizenship and rights.

The final chapter returns to the question posed in the introduction. Are we witnessing the beginning of the end of stigma associated with long-term conditions? Will illness-related stigma be consigned to history?

2 Stigma

Changing conceptual frameworks

This chapter reviews the concept of stigma and charts the diverse ways in which the concept has been defined and applied in understanding long-term illness. The key features of stigma are described and the unfolding stigma trajectory leading to the production of stigma is discussed. In particular, the chapter charts the theoretical shift from stigma as individual deviance to stigma as social oppression and shows how the stigma concept has been re-framed within a discourse of social exclusion. In the light of this reframing it considers whether stigma is still a meaningful concept or, from a theoretical perspective, it has reached its limit in terms of understanding the experience of living with a long-term condition in contemporary society.

Key facets of stigma

Conceptualizing stigma

The term 'stigma' is widely used in a number of diverse contexts as if there is a clearly defined and shared understanding about what it means. There are, however, wide discrepancies in its use and meaning. A useful and practical definition of a stigmatized group is provided by Alonzo and Reynolds in their 1995 paper 'Stigma, HIV and AIDS: an exploration and elaboration of a stigma trajectory':

> [A] category of people who are pejoratively regarded by the broader society and who are devalued, shunned or otherwise lessened in their life chances and in access to the humanizing benefit of free and unfettered social intercourse.
>
> (Alonzo and Reynolds, 1995: 304)

This definition is, broadly, the one I use in this book. It is worth at the outset, however, briefly exploring the wide variation in the conceptualization of stigma that results from the multidisciplinary backgrounds of researchers (ranging from sociologists and social psychologists through human geographers and anthropologists to political scientists) and the many diverse settings and circumstances in which stigma has been studied. 'Thus different frames of reference have led to different conceptualizations' (Link and Phelan 2001: 365) and recent literature on stigma has attempted to make sense of these differences (see Stuber, Meyer and Link, 2008).

Goffman (1963) cast stigma as a socially constructed deviance label; in the majority of studies from sociologists and social psychologists that followed, illness and disability are interpreted as social deviance and the focus is upon social interactions between the 'normal' and 'the other'. Interactions are examined in detail between those perceived as possessing discrediting attributes and those who do not and the strategies deployed by the former to retain or reclaim their status. Sociologists, rooted in the symbolic interactionist tradition, mainly focus on the social construction of stigma (Markowitz, 2005). Social psychologists are more interested in measuring and understanding prejudice, particularly how and why people construct categories and link them to stereotyped attitudes (Corrigan, 2005; Crocker, Major, and Steele, 1998). There are currently attempts to integrate these diverse disciplinary approaches (Stuber *et al*., 2008)[1] and a scholarly analysis of the commonalities and differences of the conceptual models of stigma and prejudice concludes that they are 'part of the same animal' (Phelan, Link and Dovidio, 2008: 365).

Disability theorists have criticized the focus on individuals' functional limitations and micro-level social interaction as it diverts attention away from the social environment and social oppression (Barnes and Mercer, 2003). From a 'social oppression' perspective, the focus shifts away from stigma and the individual towards processes of social exclusion and the political realities of power differentials. This shift is also being replicated in the more recent sociological literature (see Parker and Aggleton, 2003; Scambler, 2004). In response to these movements, the stigma concept has shifted dramatically and is now much broader in scope.

What is stigma?

A stigma is, literally, 'a mark branded on the skin' (Collins, 2000: 1507). For many this is a reference to the wounds of the crucified Christ and, for others, a mark burned into the skin of a slave. In social science and political discourse it denotes a, 'distinguishing mark of social disgrace' (ibid.). Beside physical marks, non-physical characteristics, such as homelessness or homosexuality, can also become objects of stigma. Both signify an individual's failure to live up to social and cultural ideals, whether by a physical blemish or by who they are – an identity. Indeed, the spoiling process associated with stigma may eclipse a person's social identity so that they are treated as belonging to a stigmatized category rather than as an individual, and devalued in the process (Zola, 1993). Such is the discomfort that it 'spoils' the social interaction and the stigmatized person becomes 'the spaz', 'the drunk' and in so doing the sense of who they are as individuals gets lost in the label.

Stigma in contemporary society is a negative construct, a mark of shame that communicates to others the fact that a person is not able to fulfil social and cultural role expectations. The origin of stigma as a failure to fulfil one's ascribed role stems largely from the work of Erving Goffman (1963) *Stigma: Notes on the Management of Spoiled Identity*.

For Goffman stigma is not an essential feature of an attribute like, for example, a visible physical mark such as a severe facial burn, but rather it emerges as a result of social reactions to such attributes. Stigma is a social product generated by social interactions in which potentially stigmatizing attributes may impact on the expectations or behaviour of either party:

> Stigma involves not so much a set of concrete individuals who can be separated into two piles, the stigmatized and the normal, as a pervasive two-role social process in which every individual participates in both roles . . . The normal and the stigmatized are not persons but rather perspectives.
>
> (Goffman, 1963: 137–8)

The discrepancy between what is expected in a 'normal' individual and what is actual in a stigmatized individual 'spoils' the social identity, through association of the stigmatizing attribute with a negative stereotype, and limits their level of social acceptance (Alonzo and Reynolds, 1995). The impact of stigma in everyday life is thus related to its inherently social nature; every day, discrediting associations are made during the stigmatized individual's social interactions.

A prerequisite of stigma then is the notion of a perceived 'difference' between what is 'normal' and what is 'other'. Stigmatization is the process by which the differential attribute is devalued and discredited and becomes synonymous with deviance so that 'we believe the person with a stigma is not quite human' (Goffman, 1963: 5).

Dimensions of stigma

Stigma varies along a number of dimensions, including degree of disruptiveness, aesthetic qualities, cause or origin, course or changes over time, the degree of peril held for others, and concealability (Jones *et al.*, 1984).

Disruptiveness, aesthetics and concealability are principally affected by the degree to which stigmatizing attributes are obvious and external, as would be the case with a visible disfigurement, as opposed to those which are hidden or internal. People with visible stigmata, such as dwarfism or acute neurofibramatosis (thought to have afflicted the so-called 'Elephant Man'), face potential disruption from all people in their social milieu (see Ablon,

1981; Ablon, 1995; Knudson-Cooper, 1981). This is also the case for those who use clearly obvious disability aids such as wheelchairs or guide dogs.

Goffman (1963) draws a useful distinction between being 'discredited' (having a visible stigma or having disclosed or been found by others to have a previously hidden one) and being 'discreditable' (possessing a hidden stigma and not disclosing it). People with hidden stigma, such as an undisclosed mental health problem or a criminal record, are discreditable. Green and Sobo (2000) show how HIV-positive people without manifest symptoms, who are therefore 'discreditable', are able to 'pass' as 'normal' and disown socially their possession of a stigmatizing attribute. However, they have to live with the possibility that people may find out about the stigmatizing attribute, and will thereby categorize them as 'discredited'.

Another key dimension of stigma relates to the origin of illness and the extent to which it is perceived to be controllable (Crocker *et al.*, 1998). Diseases that are associated with deviant behaviour, such as AIDS, which was initially, and as a result irrevocably, linked to intravenous drug use and homosexual sex, tend to elicit more stigma as people with AIDS are seen as somehow blameworthy in that they 'brought the disease upon themselves'. Likewise, drug addiction is regarded by wider society as largely avoidable and substance misusers are therefore 'blamed' for their condition.

Other key dimensions of stigma relate to the course of illness and to the perceived danger to others associated with the stigmatized condition. Illness-related disabilities that become more pronounced over time, such as multiple sclerosis when it becomes overtly symptomatic, is more discrediting and is associated with more negative societal reactions. So too are illnesses that are notably contagious, such as HIV or hepatitis C, and thus associated with putting others at risk.

A distinction is made in a study of people with epilepsy between 'enacted' and 'felt' stigma (Scambler and Hopkins, 1986).[2] Enacted stigma refers to discrimination whereby sanctions are applied to people with a condition, whereas felt or perceived stigma relates to feelings of shame and an oppressive fear of enacted stigma. In studies of people with epilepsy (Jacoby, 1994; Scambler and Hopkins, 1986), HIV-positive people (Green and Sobo, 2000) and people with severe mental illness (Green, Hayes, Dickinson, Whittaker and Gilheany, 2003), perceived stigma is more prevalent than enacted, and it predisposes the stigmatized to conceal their condition to protect themselves from experiencing discrimination.

Both perceived and enacted stigma may have severe social consequences for people in terms of their rights, freedom, self-identity and social interactions, and both may have psychopathological consequences (Jacoby, 1994) and continue for longer than the illness itself (Link, Struening, Rahav, Phelan and Nuttbrock, 1997). That perceived stigma is more prevalent than enacted may skew feelings of social restriction and discrimination.

Internalization

Antipathy towards the stigmatized does not only come from those who are 'normal'. Goffman (1963) has described how stigmatized persons incorporate and internalize the often harsh cultural standards for perfection held by the wider society of which they too are a part, and thereby discredit themselves. This is often referred to as 'self-stigma' in the literature (Corrigan and Kleinlein, 2005). Internalization of societal conceptions may lead to self-hatred and shame and a lowering of self-esteem. Negative cultural attitudes held by wider society towards stigmatized people are thus important sources of internalized stigma, and serve to pattern the individual's self-conception in a self-fulfilling manner (Williams, 1987).

The process of self-stigma is documented in a number of studies (Corrigan and Kleinlein, 2005; Green *et al.*, 2003; Link, 1987; Link and Phelan, 2001) and in powerful first-hand accounts (Estroff, 1989; Gallo, 1994). A review of these attests to the pervasiveness of self-stigma and its impact, which is associated with social withdrawal, self-devaluation, impediments to employment and social relationships and an overall sense of dehumanization (Angell, Cooke and Kovak, 2005) leading people with stigmatizing conditions such as mental illness to 'thinking of myself as garbage' (Gallo, 1994: 408).

The impact of internalizing stigma can thus lead to negative self-worth and a dramatic curtailment of life opportunities as shown, for example, in studies of people with HIV, mental illness or multiple sclerosis (Green, Hayes, Dickinson, Whittaker and Gilheany, 2002; Green and Sobo, 2000; Green and Todd, 2008). This may include non-disclosure to significant others, social withdrawal, not putting oneself forward, for example for a job, and damage to self-esteem. According to Link and Phelan (2001: 374), the stigmatized stereotype can become 'a part of a person's world view' leading to potentially 'serious negative consequences'. As a result, the stigmatized stereotype and the accompanying low self-worth are further perpetuated.

The individual's stigma can even come to dominate his or her own, and others', perceptions, and achieve what Hughes (1945) called 'master-status', which according to Schneider and Conrad (1981: 217) ' "floods" one's identity and life with meanings and behaviour that figuratively constipate the social self'.

Despite the negative consequences of self-stigma, an extensive review of social stigma by Crocker *et al.* (1998) notes that, in the main, stigmatized and oppressed groups are often able to maintain a positive view of themselves. The fact that some stigmatized people actively fight against the self-devaluation associated with self-stigma is noted as a fundamental 'paradox of self stigma' (Corrigan and Watson, 2002: 35). Whilst recognizing the negative social stereotyping associated with their condition, they respond with anger and channel these feelings into activism (Corrigan and Kleinlein, 2005).

Thus, although internalization of stigma is generally a negative process, many people have used the concept of master-status to form powerful self-help groups to further their rights to achieve political goals (see Zola, 1993), to challenge negative societal images, or to develop acceptance of a new self-identity (Ablon, 1981). This is discussed in greater detail in subsequent chapters.

The production of stigma

Having identified the principal features of stigma, let us now examine how stigma is produced. What are the key ingredients that lead to one individual or group of people stigmatizing others? Link and Phelan (2001: 363) define stigma as 'the co-occurrence of its components – labeling,[3] stereotyping, separation, status loss, and discrimination – and further indicate that for stigmatization to occur, power must be exercised'. To elaborate further, the stigma trajectory consists of the following:

- Labelling: human differences are noted and labelled.
- Stereotyping: the labels are imbued with negative stereotypes.
- Othering: labelled persons are clearly categorized as 'other' or 'them' in order to clearly separate 'them' from 'us'.
- Status loss: labelled persons are perceived by others and by themselves as devalued and inferior.
- Discrimination: labelled persons experience discrimination leading to rejection and exclusion.
- Power: stigma will only emerge if there is a clear power differential between 'us' and 'them'.

Labelling and stereotyping difference

People with a long-term condition may feel, and be regarded by others as, 'different' particularly if they are unable to, or choose not to, conceal their condition. Few children, for example, fail to stare at someone who has a prominent disfigurement. An unusually large or 'obese' woman may feel that she should not wear a bikini on the beach as it may attract unwanted attention. At its most extreme, the sense of differentness engendered by a long-term condition may lead to people avoiding social contact or being seen in public.

Sontag's (1991) work vividly illustrates how the diseased body becomes shameful through the application of metaphors which give diseases meaning. Cancer, for example, is rendered meaningful primarily through a military warfare metaphor. It is described as invasive, ruthless and predatory, breaking down defences. Through this process cancer becomes 'not just a lethal disease but a shameful one' (Sontag, 1991: 59). Other diseases acquire different types of meaning but these still serve to imbue the disease with negative meanings. Obesity becomes characterized by reference to slothful and out-of-control behaviour and the obese person is likened to a 'couch potato' and chastised for 'eating like a pig'. Metaphors are thus used to imbue conditions, and by association the person with that condition, with negative characteristics.

Labelling theory is the explanatory framework that has been developed to account for the stigmatization associated with the devalued status of people with a long-term condition (Markowitz, 2005). The process of labelling difference plays a key role in linking difference to deviance. Diseases are often linked to delinquent and deviant behaviour, particularly those like Tourette's syndrome which have symptoms that do not conform to the order and rules of public space (Davis *et al.*, 2004), or AIDS, whose transmission is seen as avoidable. HIV is characterized as an external invader and a pollutant on account of its infectivity as well as a punishment for an unhealthy lifestyle and risky behaviours (Lupton, 2003: 68). In this manner diseases become linked to deviance and the negative stereotype unfolds.

So how are labels assigned? They can be assigned by medical practitioners when, for example, a doctor diagnoses someone as having epilepsy. The wish to avoid the label that comes with a formal diagnosis may act as a barrier to seeking treatment. Labels can also be assigned by association if, for example, a person is seen attending a treatment clinic or if their medication is spotted by others. To assert more control over this process, people sometimes choose to label themselves. A campaigner speaking at a rally to raise awareness may self-disclose as being HIV positive or a 'psychiatric survivor'.

Once labelled it becomes difficult to disentangle the disease from its label. Scheff (1966), for example, shows that the label 'mentally ill' is synonymous with 'deviant' and results in society treating mental health service users as deviant when they attempt to resume their normative roles, casting them as the 'mental patient'. In turn, the labelled person internalizes this negative identity and their behaviour becomes consistent with their altered identity as they 'live up to' the label and exhibit continued deviant behaviour (known as secondary deviance). In this manner, labelling a person 'mentally ill' reinforces their deviant behaviour and leads to a spiralling career of chronic mental illness. It is part of the process by which the mentally ill person becomes socialized into the role of mental patient (Goffman, 1961).

This model of labelling theory suggests that the disabilities associated with a disease may relate more to the label than the disease itself. Whether behaviour (particularly of those labelled mentally ill) is the product of the disease or of the label has been hotly contested (Corrigan and Kleinlein, 2005; Markowitz, 2005). From a medical or 'psychiatric' perspective, it is the *behaviour* of mental health service users, which can at times be bizarre and even frightening, rather than the *label*, that leads to negative responses from the public (Gove, 1982). Gove also contests the notion that a label leads to a career of mental illness, claiming that most people perceive mental illness as a 'nervous breakdown' which 'is seen by the lay public as a transitory disorder that almost anyone might experience if they were subjected to an inordinate level of stress' (Gove, 2004: 358). By this he means that most mental health problems are not pathological but are, in the main, normal responses to stressful situations. The distress tends to be transitory, after which most people will return to their normal societal roles and function normally. They are thus able to have a negative stereotype of mental illness but not label themselves with this stereotype as they do not perceive themselves to be mentally ill. This enables them to retain a positive self-concept and lessens the stigma associated with mental health problems.

The empirical evidence offers some support for both Scheff's and Gove's positions. A study of strategies used by people with obsessive–compulsive disorder (OCD), for example, finds some support for labelling theory and some evidence against (Fennell and Liberato, 2007). All participants in this study experience OCD as chronic but many remain functional in society. Some report stigma arising as a result of their symptoms rather than the label and for some the experience of diagnosis and treatment is positive, which supports the medical view. However, there is also evidence to support the power of labelling. All feel stigmatized, internalize this stigma to varying degrees and clearly articulate that there is a discrepancy between who they are and who they want to be. All assume society has negative conceptions and adopt strategies to manage/resist stigma.

In response to the theoretical criticisms of labelling theory and the empirical evidence, a modified version of the theory, known as 'modified labelling theory', has been developed (Link, 1987; Link, Cullen, Struening, Shrout and Dohrenwend, 1989). Rather than suggesting that the label causes deviant careers, modified labelling theory offers a more subtle indirect link between the two. In this version, stereotypical attitudes towards mental illness become internalized by mental health service users. As a result they expect to be devalued and discriminated against and this then becomes a self-fulfilling prophecy. They feel demoralized, their self-esteem suffers and they may avoid social contact or choose not to seek employment in the expectation of rejection. Ultimately this leads to unemployment and social exclusion, which in turn further damages their health (Link, 1987; Link *et al.*, 1987). A number of empirical studies have provided support for modified labelling theory (e.g. Markowitz, 1998; Rosenfield, 1997) with findings which show that 'labeling and stigma indirectly leads to sustained illness' (Markowitz, 1998: 336), affecting life satisfaction and social outcomes in part through their impact on the self-concept.

The 'othering' of long-term conditions

The third component in the production of stigma is the process of 'othering'. Stereotypes are formed based upon the perceived undesirable attributes of illness such as disability, disfigurement or deviance. Such stereotypes are labelled and this labelling process forms the basis of distinctions people make between 'us' and 'them'. These distinctions are used to construct barriers to delineate the 'healthy self' from the 'unhealthy other' (see Crawford, 1994).

This process has been described in detail in relation to cultural understandings of AIDS, a disease that affected already stigmatized groups and from the outset was synonymous with physical and moral deviance, danger and contamination. In AIDS symbolism:

> The subordinate or marginalized other is culturally situated both as a physical danger to the healthy individual and as a symbolic danger to the social self. Disease in the already stigmatized other is the embodiment of moral pollution.
>
> (Crawford, 1994: 1359)

Otherness is thus a product of perceived difference and is considered dangerous because it threatens order and control (Lupton, 1999). Although the distinction between 'them' and 'us' is the basis for demarcating barriers, the delineation is not straightforward. The main danger emanating from the 'other' is that it is not only in direct opposition to self but also represents a liminal in-between mix of 'us' and 'them' – the uncertain stranger (Lupton, 2003). In this scenario, the 'other' is not a totally alien form but rather one of 'us' who has crossed a boundary, such as someone might become if abducted by aliens. The person with a long-term condition is clearly one of 'us', they may indeed be a close relative, but they have crossed the boundary from what Sontag (1991: 3) calls the 'kingdom of the well' to the 'kingdom of the sick', which makes them one of 'them' and therefore alien. Thus the apparently separate domains of insider and outsider, us and them, good and evil, the healthy and the unhealthy, are not actually separate after all.

However, people who carry a stigma are the embodiment of the ambivalent dangerous 'other.' People with a long-term condition may be treated as such, seen as polluting and contaminating, and dealt with by using exclusionary tactics to locate them both physically and symbolically as far away as possible from the self. Writes the disability theorist Jenny Morris:

> Our disability frightens people. They don't want to think that this is something which could happen to them. So we become separated from our common humanity, treated as fundamentally different and alien.
>
> (Morris, 1991: 192)

Loss of status and discrimination

Other key components of Link and Phelan's (2001) stigma trajectory are loss of status and discrimination. Loss of status for the individual with a discrediting label is a key part of the stigmatization process and has been documented and deconstructed across a range of long-term conditions. Less attention has been given to the structural aspects that underpin discriminatory behaviour following loss of status because research about stereotypes and prejudice tends to focus upon individual attitudes and cognitions (Fiske, 1998). Indeed, discrimination, related to the disadvantaged life opportunities that confront stigmatized people, is often not included in definitions of stigma in the literature (Link and Phelan, 2001).

Discrimination may operate overtly (ostracizing groups or individuals with particular labels) or covertly and indirectly. The former may involve open discrimination as in the case of a job advertisement that has as a prerequisite a requirement that the applicant be young and healthy. In the UK, most offers of employment require the applicant to complete a medical form and it is widely believed that this is used by employers to discriminate against the less healthy although technically, from a legal standpoint, it cannot be used in this manner. An example of covert discrimination is institutional racism whereby a disabling environment is created by 'processes, attitudes and behaviour which amount to discrimination through unwitting prejudice, ignorance, thoughtlessness and racist stereotyping which disadvantage minority ethnic people' (Macpherson, 1999: 28).

Stigma can also beget further stigma and this is illustrated in a study about claiming means-tested welfare benefit. This shows that people who qualify for welfare payments do not necessarily claim them and the main reason for non take-up of benefits is related to the feeling of stigma that this may engender (Page, 1984). Thus people on a low income may not seek state support because of the stigma they associate with being a welfare claimant. As a result, despite altruistic aims, the welfare system functions as an unintentional form of social control, and perpetuates stigma by reinforcing existing structural inequalities. In this sense, stigma serves as a form of social control in society.

The manner in which stigmatization of one group over another is maintained and its link to social control is well illustrated by an examination of stigma at a community level, discussed below.

The production of stigma at a community level

The literature on stigma related to chronic illness focuses primarily upon the stigmatization of individuals. However, the process of stigmatization is key to Durkheim's analysis about establishing community. By classifying those who are different as 'deviant' and a threat to the social order, stigmatization is a central part of this process and serves a function. Durkheim (1964: 68) writes, 'the establishment of a sense of community is facilitated by a class of actors who carry a stigma and are termed deviant'. 'Insiders' depend on 'outsiders' to create a boundary to delineate who belongs and who does not, so that stigma creates a boundary and a collective sense of identity and morality.

opportunities of mental health service users and finds it lacking compared with the more overtly political orientation of the disability movement. She writes, ' "Stigma" has not provided a rallying point for collective strategies to improve access or challenge prejudice. Instead the disability movement has turned to structural notions of discrimination and oppression' (Sayce, 1998: 331).

Sayce (1998) argues that the political limitations of the stigma concept are largely due to lack of definitional clarity and the multiple meanings attached to the word 'stigma' whereby the concepts of stigma, discrimination and social exclusion are often conflated. The concept of 'stigma' is used to explain both an individual's sense of shame and why stigmatized groups are disadvantaged in access to resources such as employment and housing. It has been suggested that there are more commonalities than differences between models of stigma and prejudice (Phelan *et al.*, 2008). Nevertheless, the well-documented link between stigma and individual shame tends to focus upon the 'spoiled individual' rather than the individual or collective disadvantage and exclusion that they encounter.

Sayce (1998: 341) suggests moving away from a focus on individual attitudes and attributes associated with the stigma concept and towards an examination of, and activism to redress, structural disadvantage and discrimination, defined as 'unfair treatment'. 'Unfair treatment' puts the onus of responsibility upon the perpetrator of the unfairness rather than the victim and provides a clear unambiguous rallying call for activism to combat discrimination, in much the same way as it has for black and minority ethnic groups and feminists.

Further theorizing about the link between stigma and exclusion, but from an anthropological perspective, focuses upon ideas about reciprocal exchange and 'social value' (Reidpath, Chan, Gifford and Allotey, 2005). In this model, restricted opportunities for stigmatized people (through negative health consequences and stigma) confers low 'social value' on them, which renders them less entitled to resources, thus creating and maintaining their social exclusion. In this manner, stigmatization is seen as:

> a process for controlling community membership or ensuring active social exclusion. Stigmatization is the application of the unarticulated and deeply embedded rules that govern to whom membership should be accorded – marking and separating, in crude terms, the 'in-group' from the 'out-group'.
>
> (Reidpath *et al.*, 2005: 472)

In this scenario, people with a long-term condition who are unable to work and who are restricted in their social relationships have limited 'social value', as they are a drain on resources, and become caught up in a vicious circle of stigma and exclusion. The situation will be improved only if the social structure changes to enable greater participation of the excluded, such as legislation enforcing disabled access to buildings, thus offering greater opportunities for disabled people to participate and promoting their 'social value'. Interventions should therefore focus upon promoting the 'social value' to counteract the social exclusion of stigmatized groups.

Power as a prerequisite of stigma

As noted above, the literature on stigma from both medical sociologists and social psychologists has tended to emphasize the operation of stigma at the more individual level of social interactions between the 'normal' and 'the other' and far less attention has been given to social structure (Lawton, 2003; Link and Phelan, 2001; Parker and Aggleton, 2003; Scambler, 2004).

One notable exception is a study by Ville, Ravaud, Diard and Paicheler (1994) which shows how the experience of three groups of people (people with paraplegia, people with poliomyelitis and a group without any physical impairment) is shaped by the socio-political and historical context. The illness identity of those with poliomyelitis, who developed their disabilities during the 1950s, is relatively homogeneous and largely conforms to the self-controlled and conscientious care recipient of the rehabilitation model that predominated in the 1950s. In contrast the illness identities of the more recently disabled people with paraplegia, and those with no physical impairments, are far more diverse, displaying a wide range of identities reflecting the empowerment and greater personhood associated with the current era. The illness identity, it would seem, is clearly related to the socio-political context at the time that an illness or disability develops (Ville *et al.*, 1994). According to Lawton this 'highlights the importance of locating illness experiences in 'collective' contexts that extend beyond the life and biography of the individual concerned' (Lawton 2003: 30). The need to locate the illness experience within macro-social structures is also echoed in Pierret's review of the state of knowledge in this field (Pierret, 2003).

A shift from spoiled identity towards an examination of macro structures related to social oppression, discrimination and exclusion is apparent in more recent sociological writings about stigma. Power is one of the key components in the stigmatization process outlined by Link and Phelan (2001), who argue that 'Stigma is entirely dependent on social, economic and political power – it takes power to stigmatize' (Link and Phelan, 2001: 375). Although it has been noted that successful and powerful people may also be subject to taunts, such as politicians or celebrities being pilloried in the media (see Falk, 2001), the emphasis and consequences are quite different from those associated with the stigmatization of the less powerful in that they do not result in serious discriminatory consequences.

The key role of power inequalities has long been acknowledged. The superior social capital of the 'villagers' in Elias and Scotson's study discussed earlier enabled them to dominate local politics and social relationships, which they used to maintain their superior social status in relation to residents of the 'estate'. And Page (1984: 156) notes that 'The possibility of serious conflict between stigmatizers and stigmatized serves to underlie the fact that any pattern of stigmatization is likely to further or sustain the interests of certain groups and classes at the expense of others'.

Parker and Aggleton (2003) have recently placed 'power' at the heart of their analysis of HIV-related stigma and the relative ineffectiveness of campaigns to reduce stigma. They argue that the plethora of surveys and campaigns to promote greater empathy and tolerance for HIV-positive people have had little impact in terms of increasing tolerance and understanding of wider society towards people living with HIV/AIDS. Seeking a way forward they look beyond the social interaction between stigmatized and 'normals' that has dominated stigma research, towards the structural conditions that produce social exclusion. Starting from the premise that stigma theory tends to be individualistic in nature, their analysis links the operation of stigma to power among social groups in society whereby dominant groups decide who is devalued:

> To move beyond the limitations of current thinking in this area, we need to reframe our understandings of stigmatization and discrimination to conceptualize them as social processes that can only be understood in relation to broader notions of *power* and *domination*. In our view, stigma plays a key role in producing and reproducing relations of power and control. It causes some groups to be devalued and others to feel that they are superior in some way. Ultimately, therefore, stigma is linked to the workings of *social inequality* and to properly understand issues of stigma and discrimination, whether in relation to HIV and AIDS or any other issue, requires us to think more broadly about how some individuals and groups come to be socially excluded, and about the forces that create and reinforce exclusion in different settings.
>
> (Parker and Aggleton, 2003: 16).

Drawing upon Foucault's analysis of systems such as psychiatry in which knowledge, power and control serve to mark differences between groups and bolster the power of dominant groups, they illustrate how the production of negatively valued difference, i.e. stigmatization, is linked to the creation and continuation of the social order. Extending this analysis with reference to Bourdieu's notion of hegemony, stigma is linked not only to difference but also to social and structural inequalities. They thus suggest that stigmatization is intricately linked to complex power struggles whereby individuals and groups seek to 'legitimize their own dominant status within existing structures of social inequality' (Parker and Aggleton, 2003: 18).

Adding the power element as a key ingredient in the production of stigma not only furthers understanding about the motivations and nature of those who stigmatize others but also helps to understand how the internalization of stigma leads to an oppressed identity that limits the power of the excluded and stigmatized to 'resist'. In order for the excluded to be empowered to resist and for this resistance to be used as a resource for social change, Parker and Aggleton draw upon the work of Castells and his distinction between 'legitimizing identities' introduced by dominant institutions to assert and maintain their dominance and 'resistance identities' generated by the stigmatized to challenge oppression. On the basis of this analysis, Parker and Aggleton call for structural interventions to address the socio-economic and political causes of stigma and grassroots community mobilization to actively 'resist' stigmatization and to lobby to combat inequalities.

The call to locate stigma within a broader social and economic context is also central to the recent work of Scambler (2004: 29), who argues that there is a need to 're-frame' stigma and position it more clearly within the social structure and 'axes of power'. A key contributor since the 1980s to the development of the stigma concept, he critiques his earlier analysis, which he terms the 'hidden distress model' (ibid.), about the stigma associated with epilepsy. In the hidden distress model, people with epilepsy transgress normal social interaction in two ways: first, they possess an ontological deficit, whereby they are both perceived by others and feel themselves to be 'imperfect'; second, their condition leads to disruption of social interaction through the unpredictability and 'drama' of seizures. The model is criticized on three counts: the authority it gives to the biomedical perspective; the depiction of epilepsy as 'personal tragedy'; and the focus on passivity associated with victimhood (Scambler, 2004).

This echoes the criticism of the disability theorists that interactionist accounts of stigma invariably focus upon the disruption caused by the impairment rather than upon the social environment by which impairments lead to disability (Barnes and Mercer, 2003). This inevitably leads to portrayal of the person with a long-term condition as a victim and diverts attention away from active resistance towards social oppression.

Scambler argues that, although the 'hidden distress model' still has partial validity, there is a need to move beyond such analysis in order to take greater account of the role of the social structure:

> There is potential here for a more comprehensive sociological appreciation and explanation of stigma, felt and enacted, which extends beyond traditional interactionist agendas to encompass a full range of structural antecedents and their interrelations across numerous and varied figurations.
>
> (Scambler, 2004: 40)

He is also adamant that this reframing of the stigma concept 'must include power in its remit' (ibid.: 41).

Specifically, Scambler suggests that analyses of stigmatizing conditions should be located within the post-modern political and economic climate associated with the norms of disorganized capitalism. In particular he notes that his subsequent loss of voice robbed him of his identity, commenting that 'I believe my personality to be almost entirely manifest in what I say and the way I say it' (Diamond, 1998: 168), and his changed voice left him 'feeling impotent . . . my voice was not just that of a man with a crippled throat but of one who was obviously insufficient elsewhere. I sounded, literally, disabled' (ibid.: 212). There is a perception that people are changed by long-term illness and this may impact upon their sense of belonging, sometimes even leading to social death. A young mother with cancer interviewed in France in 1960 talks about her sense of isolation, saying 'What is really so awful is that illness, I believe, really makes you very lonely . . . One is really out of the world' (Herzlich and Pierret, 1987: 178).

The concept of 'loss of self' underpins much of the literature that focuses on the subjectivity of the illness experience. Although the concept still has enormous validity and currency, there has been a discernible shift towards a reclamation of the self in the current era, whereby people with long-term conditions are often sufficiently empowered to assertively claim their rights to personhood, resources and social status. An analysis of 50 narratives of people with multiple sclerosis, for example, identifies only five that clearly embody the 'loss of self' perspective (Robinson, 1990). Those with long-term illnesses can now negotiate alternative identities as 'survivors' and dis-associate themselves from the 'victims' associated with loss of self (see for example Crossley, 1997). And there are the many service users who become increasingly involved in their health and social care as the 'expert patient' is introduced into systems of care (Taylor and Bury, 2007). What is key about such empowerment is that it is based upon and reinforces selfhood, albeit a self that has been developed and refashioned in response to illness, but not one that has been lost.

From 'biographical disruption' to 'biographical flow' and the growth of the remission society

A key concept in the medical sociology literature based upon the 'insider' perspective of the illness experience is that of 'biographical disruption', which refers to a disruption of one's expected life trajectory in response to a diagnosis with a chronic illness (Bury, 1982). Bury highlights the complex and multifaceted ways in which the experience of chronic illness can lead to a fundamental rethinking of a person's biography and self-concept.

Chronic illness and its associated symptoms can disrupt everyday life and introduce a sense of uncertainty about the future, particularly around the time of diagnosis. The impact of long-standing symptoms on everyday life disrupts one's sense of the taken-for-granted world, and may require a reordered lifestyle and a reappraisal of one's life trajectory. Bury (1991) identifies two types of 'meaning' associated with chronic illness which account for this disruption. The first is the consequences of the illness in terms of how symptoms and treatment regimes impact upon everyday life. The second is the significance of illness that may affect people's sense of self and how others see them. This may entail a renegotiation of identity involving a changed biography, altered relationships and a changed sense of self. Mathieson and Stam (1995), who interviewed people with cancer, conceptualize this as 'disrupted feelings of fit' (ibid.: 293), which refers to a person's changed social role and the renegotiation of identity that takes place between people diagnosed with a chronic illness and their social environment. As one of Mathieson and Stam's participants said, 'I suppose to my friends I'm Ruth with cancer, not just plain Ruth' (ibid.: 294), and another reported a process whereby the illness is objectified and the person with cancer is seen 'as a tumour, not as a person' (ibid.: 296). The disruption that chronic illness entails may then require 'biographical work' to recraft one's identity in the light of having a long-term condition as individuals try to find 'explanations that make sense in terms of their life circumstances and biographies . . . and reestablish credibility in the face of the assault on self-hood which is involved' (Bury, 1991: 456).

The concept of 'biographical disruption' has however been critiqued and developed from a number of perspectives. Disability theorists, such as Oliver (1996a), reject the concept as it is grounded in the limitations of the impaired body, which is seen as a source of 'personal tragedy', and deflects attention from the limitations of a society that disables disabled people.

Williams (2000) turns the idea of illness leading to biographical disruption around and looks at 'biographical disruption as chronic illness' whereby altered life-events such as losing a job or death of a close family member may play a role in the aetiology of long-term illness. As evidence, he draws upon two narratives of people with rheumatoid arthritis, one of whom locates the cause of their illness in 'workplace toxicity' and the other in a 'web of stressful events and processes', that is, for both it was '*biographical disruption which triggered their illness*' (ibid.: 52). He cites studies that link severe life-events to the onset of a range of mental health problems and psychosocial causes of health inequalities as further evidence.

Within this wider theoretical critique a number of empirical studies have challenged the notion of 'biographical disruption' as an inevitable corollary of chronic illness. People with long-term illnesses are numerous and diverse, characterized by their heterogeneity, and the onset of illness is not necessarily 'biographically disruptive' for all. Facets of a person prior to onset of illness, such as stage in the life-course, will mediate the impact of illness. Illnesses linked to congenital conditions that are present from birth or early childhood cannot be said to disrupt a biography when they 'are integral to an individual's biographically embodied self' (Williams, 2000: 50).

Studies of older people recovering from stroke show how former life experiences and age may mediate the impact of illness so that biographies are not 'inevitably disrupted' and some people 'maintain a sense of a coherent pre- and post-stroke self' (Faircloth, Boylstein, Rittman, Young, and Gubrium, 2004: 244). A study of 57 US military veterans aged 46 to 88 years marginalized, the emergence of identity politics and the expression of the social model of disability. This results in politicization at three levels: individual identity, social or interpersonal, and governmental. Shakespeare and Watson cite the deaf community, who began organizing as a social movement in the 1970s, as an example. They challenged their status as disabled, casting themselves instead as a linguistic minority, using slogans such as 'Deaf Pride' to assert their identity. The emergent deaf identity went hand in hand with their political mobilization, which culminated in the US with the successful 'Deaf President Now' protest in 1988 to force the Board of Trustees of Gallaudet University, a university for the deaf, to reverse its decision to appoint a hearing president.

Consciousness-raising among people living with long-term conditions is now well established and has resulted in action against discriminatory treatment and demand for respect and rights. Anspach's study of political activism among 'former mental patients' and people with disabilities in the 1970s conceptualizes this as a shift 'from stigma to identity politics' (Anspach, 1979: 765). The social movements linked to identity politics seek to alter both self- and societal conceptions about illness and disability. They are fundamentally different from the former voluntary organizations that were traditionally led by advocates of the sick and disabled rather than the sick themselves and also different from self-help groups, which were therapeutic in orientation. They are overtly polemical and political, openly seeking legislative change, opposing discrimination and frequently using 'demonstrations and the tactics of social protest' (ibid.: 766). Political action thus challenges popular conceptions of people with long-term conditions as helpless and powerless and, in this manner, 'political goals and strategies often become a vehicle for the symbolic manipulations of the persona and the public presentation of self' (ibid.).

This assertive stance challenges societal notions of how long-term sick and disabled people should behave. The new assertiveness of those with long-term conditions sits uneasily with traditional theoretical sociologies of deviance that cast the long-term ill as passive and powerless patients whose identity or 'label' is imposed upon them. According to Anspach, 'The politicization of the disabled represents an attempt to wrest definitional control of identity from "normals"' (ibid.: 768). It therefore represents a fundamental challenge to the stigmatization associated with their condition, and one that militates against stereotypical societal categorizations. Not only does it lead to political action and change but it also offers a form of resistance against 'incorporating definitions of helplessness and passivity into their self-conceptions' (ibid.). The political and the personal are thus intertwined.

The link between self-identity and political action is characteristic of many new social movements and lies at the heart of the disability movement and the majority of the diverse social movement organizations that have emerged from it. Charlton (1998) identifies 10 different types of disability rights organizations ranging from local self-help groups often based on a single issue or impairment to national coalitions of disabled people to international organizations. In addition to these activist networks there are a range of 'second wave' organizations involved in support and service delivery, many of which have radical roots in that they emerged from political activism, but gradually have become incorporated into mainstream service provision (Shakespeare and Watson, 2001).

In terms of an exploration of the erosion of stigma, it is worth listing the essential elements of identity politics and the strategies of health and disability movements. First is the recognition of the legitimacy of the illness experience and the negotiation of positive illness identities. The creative and potential personal growth aspects of illness are emphasized. The language that is adopted stresses abilities rather than disabilities so that derogatory terms such as 'cripples' are replaced by terms such as 'wheelchair users'.

Second is the shift in the concept of disability and illness from being viewed as an individual medical problem to a social and political issue (Barnes and Mercer, 2003). Increasingly, the central problems of illness and disability are located not in individual pathology but in an unjust culture of political, economic and social exclusion. Personal problems become transformed into social issues. As a result, stigmatization is seen as a product of, and problem for, society rather than the individual. In this manner the collective illness identity is linked to a broader social critique, and shared grievances, such as discrimination or lack of access to treatment, lead to 'the development of a politicized collective illness identity' (Brown *et al.*, 2004: 62). These processes have coalesced around the notion of rights.

Third is the challenge to medical dominance in the definition and treatment of illness and disability. The traditional passive patient has become increasingly assertive in the medical encounter (Lupton, 2003). They may consult the vast array of information about medical conditions on the internet and are increasingly well informed about their condition, enabling them to negotiate treatment with their doctor rather than passively following 'doctor's orders'. Radicalized mental health service users, disaffected by medical dominance, may even show disdain for psychiatric authorities and reject the range of antipsychotic and antidepressant drugs prescribed for them. In addition, a growing number of those living with long-term conditions seek alternative therapies that have their origin in non-western, 'folk' or 'new age' traditions as an alternative to, or to complement, biomedical treatment.

There are clear limits and barriers to identity politics and the ethos of empowerment has itself been problematized. Crossley's study of HIV-positive individuals shows that, whereas they embraced empowerment and questioned medical authority in the light of their experiential expertise and claimed their sexual and reproductive rights to remain sexually active and have children, they were less willing to assume responsibility to minimize the spread of infection. Crossley (1998: 528) interprets this as evidence of 'inherent and implicit contradictions of the increasingly popular discourse disability is a source of pride and empowerment – a symbol of enriched self-identity and self-worth and a central force coalescing a community intent on extolling the fundamental values of life, human rights, citizenship, and the celebration of difference.

(Albrecht, Seelman and Bury, 2001: 1–2)

There is a changed consciousness among those with long-term conditions and increased opportunities to negotiate for equal rights and full citizenship.

The following chapters draw upon empirical data relating to three specific conditions to explore in more detail the workings of the three challenges to stigma associated with long-term conditions.

4 The technological challenge to stigma
HIV and the advent of HAART

This chapter examines the technological challenge and focuses exclusively upon HIV, a condition that has been transformed as a result of technological advances in the form of effective pharmaceutical therapy, which has had a dramatic impact upon the experience of living with HIV.

AIDS in the late twentieth century had all the key ingredients associated with stigma. It was a new disease about which little was known, there was no cure, it was infectious, acquisition was associated with a number of stigmatized behaviours and, in the western world, it mainly affected already stigmatized groups. HIV unleashed what was termed 'an epidemic of stigma' (Herek and Glunt, 1988: 886).

After documenting the nature of HIV-related stigma this chapter examines the impact of the introduction of highly active antiretroviral therapy (HAART),[1] which became available in 1996 to HIV-positive people living in more affluent countries. The chapter focuses upon those who have ready access to HAART who, as a result, are living longer, healthier lives and re-entering the labour market and engaging with activities of daily living. This process has been termed 'normalization' in that HIV is now one of many chronic illnesses and it is treated as such in public health policy (Moatti and Souteyrand, 2000). Here I explore whether this process of 'normalization' is matched, or at least echoed, by development and change in the wider social world. To what extent has HAART had an impact on the stigmatization experienced by HIV-positive people?

The chapter draws heavily upon two studies I conducted related to HIV.[2] The first was a longitudinal study of 66 HIV-positive people living in Scotland whom I interviewed between 1990 and 1994. It was a heterogeneous sample comprising men and women who belonged to a number of so-called HIV risk groups, including gay men, people with haemophilia, injecting drug users, as well as a small number of people infected through heterosexual intercourse. The study focused upon the psychosocial impact of living with what was then a relatively new and unknown disease with no cure or effective treatment (see Green and Sobo, 2000). The second study involved a comprehensive review of the published and unpublished 'grey' literature has to be balanced with experiencing unpleasant side effects (Flowers, Imrie, Hart and Davis, 2003). A gay man taking HAART describes his life as being 'in limbo . . . a compromise between side effects and an HIV regimen that seems to be keeping me alive; a process of sustaining a body that will never be well, but may very well continue to be' (Goldman, 2003: 5). In some case, the side effects may be of such severity that continuation is intolerable (Brashers *et al.*, 1999).

The side effects that perhaps cause most concern are the metabolic disorders lipodystrophy and lipoatrophy (Persson, 2004), often referred to as HIV-related adipose redistribution syndrome (HARS). This syndrome relates to the redistribution of body fat and can result in a changed body shape. Lipodystrophy and lipoatrophy usually occur together. The former refers to an increase in waist and breast size and/or pronounced fat gain around the back of the neck and upper back, and the latter to wasting on the face, especially the cheeks. Prevalence of HARS has been difficult to determine largely because of definitional problems but a review of 15 published surveys of HIV-positive people suggests a prevalence of 9 per cent to 48 per cent (mean 32 per cent), the variance being largely related to the criteria used to define the syndrome (Lichtenstein *et al.*, 2004).

The changes in body shape associated with HARS may result in a loss of control over disclosure. Indeed it has been compared to Kaposi's Sarcoma, an illness associated with AIDS that produces visible lesions on the body, which was common in the pre-HAART era. Lipodystrophy and lipoatrophy can lead to involuntary disclosure of HIV in that they are visible identifiers of HIV and may project one's HIV status into the public domain, particularly within gay communities where the physical signs of HARS are likely to be well known.

A number of cosmetic surgery procedures are available to redress the undesired bodily changes attributed to HARS (see AIDSmeds 2006). These involve a process of fat transfer and include liposuction to remove unwanted fat from the abdomen, breasts or back of the neck, and implants of fat or fat substitutes injected or surgically implanted into the face. The latter procedure is known as 'New Fill' and masks the effects of lipoatrophy on the face by 'filling out' the trademark hollows caused by the loss of facial fat (Valantin *et al.*, 2003). There are risks associated with such surgical procedures and the changes may not last but, according to one cosmetic surgeon, 'The change is so dramatic that they look 10 to 20 years younger. They look like themselves again' (American Society for Plastic Surgeons, 2004).

HARS can have a negative impact on self-esteem and quality of life especially among those who are younger and newly diagnosed (Power, Tate, McGill and Taylor, 2003). It may affect social interaction and communication as it is associated with loss of control over disclosure, reduced sexual attractiveness and reduced facial expression (Persson and Newman, 2006), which can lead to reduced social contact and isolation (Power *et al.*, 2003). Bodily changes may impact on reactions of others towards the HIV-positive person and affect their own sense of identity (Persson, 2003). According to a black African[7] woman living in the UK:

> You know the way a woman move, a woman is proud of the way she looks, you know a small waist, nice bum, nice legs and suddenly that's all taken away from you. And in a case where you haven't disclosed your status and people start seeing the body changing – that alone is enough to disclose your status.
>
> (cited in Flowers *et al.*, 2006: 116)

Impact of the technological challenge

Participation and inclusion

HAART has had a profound impact on the illness trajectory and transformed the experience of those HIV-positive people who take the medication. In countries where the majority of the population have access to HAART, mortality and morbidity rates have fallen, specialist AIDS wards in hospitals and AIDS hospices have closed and many AIDS service organizations have been unable to secure funding as HIV is no longer considered high priority. AIDS is now viewed as a manageable chronic illness (Catalan, Green and Thorley, 2003; Siegel and Lekas, 2002) and media representations of HIV-positive people, which had formerly emphasized illness and death with images of cadaverous patients, now portray HIV as a manageable long-term condition. Such a transformation has not yet occurred in many less developed countries where access to antiretrovirals is limited due to lack of resources and AIDS remains a terminal illness associated with greatly reduced life expectancy. However, in western countries such as the UK, HIV in the twenty-first century is described in popular culture as 'the forgotten disease' because 'people don't worry about HIV anymore' (Stephen Fry in the TV documentary *HIV and Me* on BBC2, 2 October 2007).

When HAART first become available, the improvement in health associated with taking it was so marked that it was described as a 'Lazarus Phenomenon' (e.g. Thompson, 2003). Studies measuring quality of life in a number of domains reported improvements, in contrast to longitudinal research in the pre-HAART era, which reported deterioration in all areas of quality of life (Saunders and Burgoyne, 2002). In the literature on the experience of HIV there was a perceptible shift from concerns about illness and dying to the problems of living and, for some, actively re-engaging with society (Green and Smith, 2004).

Improvements in health enabled many HIV-positive people, even those at a relatively late stage of the illness, to re-engage with mainstream life. Prior to the development of HAART it was estimated that 45 to 65 per cent of HIV-positive people in the US, Europe and Australia were unemployed (Dray-Spira and Lert, 2003). Post-HAART, many who had stopped working reported feeling well enough to return to work although there were a number of barriers to overcome (Maticka-Tyndale, Adam and Cohen, 2002). These included returning to the labour market after a long absence; concern about having the flexibility to attend to medical needs; worry about disclosure, stigma and discrimination; and concern that disability benefits might be lost (Ferrier and Lavis, 2003).

Notwithstanding such barriers, a far greater proportion of HIV-positive people are able to participate in the labour market than hitherto. And in the UK they are offered some support from the Disability Discrimination Act of 1995, which prohibits discrimination against those who have a disability and this now includes all HIV-positive people from the point of diagnosis.

The improved health and prognosis associated with HAART also has an impact upon sexual and social relationships. The extended survival associated with HAART has implications for long-term personal relationships which can now be established with the prospect of a long-term future (Brashers *et al.*, 1999).[8] Maintaining safe sexual behaviour long-term may be difficult, particularly for those who look and feel well. It is also widely perceived that use of HAART reduces risk of HIV transmission as the viral load is reduced (Kalichman, Nachimson, Cherry and Williams, 1998). This perception of reduced risk linked to a low or undetectable viral load has been noted in a number of diverse populations and may be linked to less safe sexual behaviour (Brashers *et al.*, 1999; Chinouya and Davidson, 2003; Davis *et al.*, 2002). In addition, the notion that HIV is a manageable disease may also contribute to a reduction in safe sexual behaviour (Siegel and Lekas, 2002).

Uncertainty remains a feature of HIV (Brashers *et al.*, 2003), but hope for the future is nevertheless identified as a key theme in the post-HAART era (Anderson and Weatherburn, 1998; Fernandez, 2001; Lee *et al.*, 2002) and the emphasis has shifted to the problems associated with living rather than dying with HIV. The mental health concerns of HIV-positive people have changed from acute problems associated with dying to complex chronic problems associated with the ongoing demands of daily life (Catalan, Meadows and Douzenis, 2000). For example, in the UK for many HIV-positive people, particularly those from some migrant groups, concern about poverty is more salient and acute than concern about HIV. For many HIV-positive black Africans, for example, problems relating to income, housing or immigration are often of greater concern than HIV and 'within this range of stressful life circumstances, HIV is only one of many problems, and tellingly it is not thought of as *the* most important' (Flowers *et al.*, 2006: 113). An HIV diagnosis is only one facet of life and may have a lower priority than the everyday struggle to survive.

Thus the impact of HIV has become relatively marginal to a number of HIV-positive people, expressed by a gay man who took part in 'The Sexual Health and Anti-Retroviral Project' as 'Do we need to be so HIV with ourselves?' (Davis *et al.*, 2000). And a HIV-positive gay man with no drug-related side effects claimed, 'I don't think of myself as having HIV any more. I have functionally forgotten that I've got it' (cited in the Stephen Fry documentary *HIV and Me* on BBC2, 2 October 2007).

It is clear that HIV-positive people with access to HAART have greater opportunities for social and economic participation and the next section considers the extent to which this has led to a decrease in stigma, social exclusion and discrimination.

Social exclusion and discrimination

Discrimination and social exclusion are still associated with HIV; this is not only related to the stigma of HIV but is also because HIV disproportionately affects people living in more marginalized and vulnerable circumstances. The epidemiology shows that HIV is ever more strongly associated with poverty and disadvantage (Dray-Spira and Lert, 2003). Over 66 per cent of HIV-positive people are in sub-Saharan Africa, an area that ranks highest on poverty indices such as GDP and literacy levels, and more than 96 per cent of new HIV infections in 2007 were in low- and middle-income countries (UNAIDS/WHO, 2007). And in more affluent countries such as the UK, HIV is increasingly clustered among more disadvantaged communities such as ethnic minority groups (Green and Smith, 2004). Thus poverty and social exclusion are increasingly associated with HIV and there is also some evidence that social exclusion are exacerbated through the experience of HIV (Atrill, Kinniburgh, and Power, 2001).

Social inequalities associated with HIV are further compounded by the fact that access to HAART is highly correlated with relative wealth. In lower- and middle-income countries, only a small proportion of HIV-positive people have access to antiretrovirals despite initiatives to reduce prices of western pharmaceuticals and less expensive generic manufacture of HAART (Hosseinipour, Kazembe, Sanne and van der Horst, 2002). In the main AIDS remains a terminal disease in developing countries.[9]

There is evidence of widespread stigma directed at HIV-positive people throughout the world and efforts to combat the negative effects of HIV/ AIDS-related stigma are identified as key challenges by the World Health Organization's Global Programme on AIDS and the United Nations Programme on HIV/AIDS (Parker and Aggleton, 2003).

Studies of public attitudes suggest that HIV-related stigma is still relatively widespread. A telephone survey of the general population in the US compared AIDS stigma in 1991 and 1999. Even though overt expressions of stigma declined, in 1999 one-third of the sample still expressed negative feelings towards HIV-positive people and almost one-half felt that people with AIDS were responsible for their illness (Herek, Capitanio and Widaman, 2002).

Findings from a British survey confirm that, although attitudes about HIV have become a little more liberal, the underlying stigma related to blame and risk of contagion of HIV remains firmly entrenched (National AIDS Trust,

2008). A survey based upon a representative sample of British people aged over 16 compared attitudes in 2007 with those in earlier years (2005 and 2000 but not, unfortunately, before HAART) (ibid.). A high proportion (69 per cent) agree that 'there is a great deal of stigma in the UK today around HIV and AIDS'. This, however, represents a significant and steady decline since 2000, suggesting that some people at least, particularly in younger age groups, perceive that the stigma is somewhat reduced. Although declining, the proportion who perceive HIV/AIDS to be a stigmatized condition nevertheless remains high and 71 per cent agree that 'more needs to be done to tackle prejudice against people living with HIV' (ibid.).

The notion that HIV-positive people are often to blame for their infection remains relatively entrenched, particularly among older people and those with no formal qualifications. Almost half (47 per cent) of the sample agree that 'people who become infected with HIV through unprotected sex have only themselves to blame' and this increases to 65 per cent who agree that those infected through drug use have only themselves to blame. The proportion expressing these views declined in 2005 in comparison with 2000 but increased in 2007, suggesting no marked trend over time with respect to the blame aspect of HIV stigma. In Britain, HIV still retains the 'double stigma' due to the association with marginalized groups such as gay men, drug users and more recently African communities (Kinniburgh, Scott, Gottlieb and Power, 2001).

Over two-thirds of those people surveyed said that if they found out that a neighbour or someone in their family had HIV the relationship would not be damaged (National AIDS Trust, 2008). A similar proportion agreed that 'people with HIV deserve the same level of support and respect as someone with cancer'. However, another study comparing the impact of stigma upon people with cancer and those with HIV found that HIV-positive people reported stronger feelings of stigma than people with cancer (Fife and Wright, 2000).

The British survey also reported that 70 per cent said that they would be comfortable working with an HIV-positive colleague and 70 per cent also agreed that 'most people with HIV these days can work like everyone else'. Both these proportions are higher than they were in 2005, suggesting that there is a greater expectation that HIV-positive people will join the workforce and greater acceptance towards them when they do.

Thus the overall picture of public attitudes in Britain suggests some reduction in stigma but the change is not very marked and there remains a sizeable minority (about a third) who profess to hold pejorative views towards HIV-positive people.

There is also evidence that living with HIV is associated with a number of restrictions in terms of travel, immigration and work. A total of 74 countries are reported to have some form of HIV-specific travel restrictions and 12 ban entry for any reason (UNAIDS, 2008). In the US, for example, visa law requires people who are HIV-positive to apply for a special waiver to travel there. Although people are not tested for HIV when they enter the US, all non-US citizens must get a visa to enter legally. In the summer 2005 a gay immigration group called Immigration Equality reported that Fernando Pena, a gay Argentinian actor, was denied a visa renewal by US authorities because he was HIV positive. Those who do not disclose their HIV status on their visa application may be deported on arrival if they are found to be HIV positive – if, for example, their HAART medication is discovered. HIV-positive people also face restriction regarding working or migrating to other countries such as the United Arab Emirates, where anyone over the age of 18 who applies for a work and residence permit is required to take a medical exam including an HIV test, which must be conducted in the Emirates. Those who test HIV positive are deported. And in Australia, HIV testing was introduced in 1989 for all migrants aged 15 or older. Applicants diagnosed as positive for HIV/AIDS are not automatically refused entry but the condition is investigated to estimate potential costs. There is evidence that at least some applicants are refused entry (City Press, 2005) and a number of countries have similar restrictions (Garmaise, 2002). According to Dr Peter Piot, Executive Director of UNAIDS:

> No other condition prevents people from entering countries for business, tourism, or to attend meetings. No other condition has people afraid of having their baggage searched for medication at the border, with the result that they are denied entry or worse, detained and then deported back to their country.
>
> (UNAIDS, 2008)

HIV-positive people may face discrimination in the workplace, although there is some protection thanks to the 1995 Disability Discrimination Act. In the UK, Scott Watts was sacked from his job as a carer in October 2004 after telling his employers he was HIV positive. His employers deemed that Scott posed a major risk to their clients, young men with challenging behaviour, as there was a likelihood Scott could be bitten by clients who could then become infected. He appealed and the case was taken to an employment tribunal, which upheld his claim of disability-related discrimination (O'Connor, 2005).

Taking action against such discrimination is however relatively rare. In one study, 84 per cent of HIV-positive people reported discrimination but because of concerns or lack of knowledge about the legal process, lack of funds and fears about confidentiality only 4 per cent considered legal action (Sherr, Sherr and Orchard, 1998).

There are also restrictions upon HIV-positive workers performing some procedures in the workplace. In the UK, for example, HIV-positive health care workers have to disclose their HIV status to their employer's occupational health department and are not able to perform any exposure-prone procedures (known as 'bleed-back') whereby injury to the health care worker could result in the worker's blood contaminating the patient's open tissues (Department of Health, 2005).

Stigma continues to feature as a major issue in studies of HIV-positive people globally and is reported to be very pronounced in studies of HIV-positive people living in lower- and middle-income countries such as South Africa (Hosegood, Preston-Whyte, Busza, Moitse and Timaeus, 2007) and China (Zhou, 2007). Stigma also remains a concern of HIV-positive people with access to HAART, particularly among some groups, such as black Africans living in the UK (Green and Smith, 2004). A study of African women living in the UK reported that HIV-related stigma has a profound impact on their lives, with one-third reporting direct experience of HIV-related stigmatization such as rejection by partners, and a further third reporting anxieties about fear of discrimination (Anderson and Doyal, 2004).

Disclosure of HIV status a key concern

There is a clear association between stigma and disclosure about being HIV-positive whereby fear of negative reactions from others acts as a deterrent to disclose (Flowers *et al.*, 2006; Green and Sobo, 2000; Mayfield Arnold, Rice, Flannery and Rotheram-Borus, 2008; Petrak, Doyle, Smith, Skinner, and Hedge, 2001). Whereas the meaning of disclosure has changed since the advent of HAART, as it no longer denotes progressively declining health and a shortened life-span, the actual process of disclosure does not appear to have changed in response to this. This, perhaps, reflects the fact that negative attitudes towards HIV-positive people, despite showing some decline, are still firmly entrenched in a sizeable minority of the population.

Disclosure among some groups remains very low indeed. Studies of black Africans living in Britain report that, although over 80 per cent who are HIV positive disclose to someone, the people most likely to be told are health care professionals (Anderson and Doyal, 2004; Chinouya and Davidson, 2003; Weatherburn, Ssanyu-Sseruma, Hickson, McLean and Reid, 2003). Non-disclosure means that social support is less forthcoming and can lead to social isolation. The quote below from a black African woman in her early twenties living in London shows how isolated people can become:

> I don't have any friends, I rarely go out. The only person I ever talk to about HIV or anything is my consultant when I go to see him about my blood: that's the only time I ever get to talk about it. After that I just go back to trying to lock myself up in my little world until the next meeting, and that's it.
>
> (cited in Flowers *et al.*, 2006: 115)

Decisions about whether and whom to tell are rarely straightforward. Some decide to tell nobody, others tell everybody, although this latter group still have to decide when and how to tell people and how much information to disclose. The majority, however, choose a pathway between these two extremes and tell some people in some circumstances. Disclosure is generally prompted by a need for support or a feeling of duty to inform others and non-disclosure is primarily related to fear of discriminatory treatment and/ or rejection (Mayfield Arnold *et al.*, 2008). These factors appear to have changed little since the pre-HAART era (see Green and Sobo, 2000; Hays *et al.*, 1993).

Rates of disclosure are very difficult to determine from the published literature as they vary significantly according to cultural context, social characteristics of the HIV-positive person and how disclosure is 'measured'. A review of articles on disclosure of heterosexual adults (mainly but not exclusively based on US populations) found that rates were higher among women than men; younger than older people; latino and white than African-American families (Mayfield Arnold *et al.*, 2008). Rates of disclosure to primary sexual partners and family members were relatively high but lower in non-western countries and much lower to secondary or casual sexual partners. Disclosure to employers was 27–68 per cent and up to 40 per cent did not disclose to health care professionals. Although difficult to compare, the overall trends suggest that disclosure rates have not changed markedly with the advent of HAART (see Green and Sobo, 2000; Hays *et al.*, 1993). Social characteristics, context and role relationships explained more of the variance in disclosure rates than access to effective treatment (Mayfield Arnold *et al.*, 2008).

It is clear that disclosure remains a key issue facing HIV-positive people in the post-HAART era. A recent report based upon findings from focus groups involving over 600 people and organized by the UK Coalition of People Living with HIV and AIDS identifies disclosure in a number of domains as a central concern of people living with HIV (National AIDS Trust, 2007). Concern is expressed that a patient's HIV-positive status may not be treated with sufficient confidentiality in health care settings and confidentiality is also an issue in shared housing, primarily on account of a lack of privacy for storing and taking medication. The main concern about employment also relates to the issue of whether to disclose HIV status to employers, how to explain gaps in employment history and any possible legal implications that may be related to non-disclosure (ibid.).

Legal implications about non-disclosure are particularly keenly felt in sexual relationships. In some countries, such as the UK, there is the threat of a custodial sentence if a HIV-positive person conceals their HIV status, fails to use condoms consistently and infects a partner. If the partner decides to make a complaint to the police, they can be prosecuted for reckless transmission. There have been several successful prosecutions so far for the sexual transmission of HIV (Bird and Leigh-Brown, 2001; Weait and Azad, 2005). The alternative is to disclose to sexual partners but this entails dealing with the social consequences of doing so, particularly as sexual relationships can be volatile and dissolve acrimoniously. Thus disclosure and non-disclosure both have risks attached and the decision may need to be carefully weighed up according to circumstances.

Is an 'HIV identity' less pronounced?

The prevalence of symptoms has declined with HAART and therefore HIV has less physical impact and is less 'visible', thus potentially making it less salient to the identity and self-concept of HIV-positive people. The man quoted earlier in this chapter who '[doesn't] think of myself as having HIV any more', clearly categorizes himself as both physically and morally 'healthy'. The change in identity is marked.

Health can be seen as a key marker of identity and an HIV-positive person before HAART was characterized as the embodiment of the 'unhealthy other' (Crawford, 1994: 1347). For Crawford the pursuit of health and the pursuit of moral personhood are intertwined and the immune system lies at the heart of the individual's control over their body so that 'a compromised immunity is a compromised self' (ibid.: 1358). A malfunctioning immune system is thus associated with a lack of control, diminished responsibility and immorality.

Taking HAART helps to restore the immune system and, in so doing, one would in theory expect the restoration of the moral worthy self. The increased participation of HIV-positive people in social and economic life suggests that this may be occurring in that it denotes not only improved health but also enhanced self-esteem. However, the side effects of antiretroviral medication may counteract the improvements to self-identity associated with a bolstered immune system. The use of efavirenz, an anti-HIV drug that reduces the amount of virus in the body, may result in insomnia and mental health disorders such as depression, psychosis and suicidal ideation. This presents a paradox, and the emergence of 'troubled selves' (Persson and Newman, 2006: 1594), in that the treatment simultaneously bolsters the self by strengthening the immune system and attacks the self through side effects that may threaten a person's sense of balance and self-identity.

This paradox is also observed with the side effect HARS as the redistribution of body fat may have a very negative impact on self-image (Persson, 2004). Thus many of those taking HAART may still self-identify as 'unhealthy' and therefore 'other'. According to Richard Goldman, a gay man taking HAART, 'The loss of my identity continues to be profound. I returned to a job, only to fail within days. I had to let go of that part of my life' (Goldman, 2003: 6).

An HIV diagnosis continues to be a life-changing experience (Rosengarten *et al.*, 2004), and one that may have a profound impact upon identity. 'The drama of identity construction' identified among gay men with AIDS in the late 1980s (Sandstrom, 1990: 271) remains a challenge for HIV-positive people in the twenty-first century. One black African woman for example refers to the day she received her HIV diagnosis as her 'real birthday', as it heralded the beginning of a total change in her life:

> Interviewer: And I guess you feel that you always remember that date?
> R: You don't forget. I call it my real birthday, yeah.
> Interviewer: Why do you call it that?
> R: Because my life took a totally different perspective. It's like being, I don't know what it means to be born again, but it's like being born again, you know. You don't ever look at life in the same way, you know. My life took a totally different perspective.

(cited in Flowers et al., 2006: 117)

However, studies about adjustment to HIV post-HAART emphasize strategies that are used to reaffirm moral personhood (Crossley, 1997; Ezzy, 2000; Stanley, 2003). There is also evidence that HIV-positive people's sense of self worth overcomes their perception of having a stigmatized condition (Fife and Wright, 2000). This suggests that HAART is associated with enhanced physical health and self-image. In addition, HIV is not necessarily the most salient aspect in the lives of HIV-positive people, or of their identity. Thus, 'the drama of identity construction' would appear to be less apparent among HIV-positive people than in the pre-HAART era.

To what extent has HAART challenged stigma?

New technology has improved the health of HIV-positive people and is associated with their greater participation in social and economic life. There is also a small but nevertheless discernible shift in public attitudes. However, a sizeable minority of the population continues to hold very negative views towards HIV-positive people and believe that they are largely to blame for their illness. This means that disclosure still needs to be actively managed, and the social fear evoked by an HIV diagnosis is well illustrated by the bizarre story of Alberto Zabbialini, an Italian man who when diagnosed as HIV positive fled his home and lived a hermit's life in the Ligurian woods. He re-emerged only three months later when he went to an internet café and read articles about himself saying that the test result was a mistake and he was perfectly healthy (*Daily Mail*, 2007). HIV/AIDS remains a stigmatized condition.

Although the technology has had only a limited impact in terms of addressing the underlying causes of HIV-related stigma, it has nevertheless challenged stigma by enabling many HIV-positive people to mask their illness much more effectively, thus making HIV less salient to their public identity. The ability of HAART to control progression of HIV has caused a marked change in terms of concealment.

and it has been argued that among young people drug use has become so normalized that non-acquaintance with drugs or drug users has become the deviation from the norm (Parker, Measham and Aldridge, 1995).

The majority of people who use substances, including many of those who are heavy users, do not experience negative social effects relating to their use and continue to lead relatively 'normal lives'. Gossop (2007), for example, cites the case of Dr William Stewart Halstead, the founder of the prestigious Johns Hopkins Medical School in the US, who, despite a large daily dose of morphine, gained an international reputation. A similar figure has been created in the US medical drama *House* featuring Dr House whose brilliance as a diagnostician appears to be associated with his dependence on Diconal, an opioid-based pain killer. Substance misusers, however, by definition experience disruption to their lives and may disrupt the lives of others.

There is ongoing unresolved debate about whether substance misusers are sinners or sick; accordingly they are treated with either punishment or support or sometimes both. With the onset of HIV and AIDS, the notion of harm reduction to reduce transmission of HIV infection through sharing needles gained ascendancy. Since this time substance misuse treatment has increasingly been brought within the care system and the condition has been treated as pathological. Hence the inclusion of substance misusers in this book on long-term conditions.

Substance misusers: deviant and dangerous

Drugs and deviance

The stereotype of the 'junkie' or 'dope fiend' is a powerful image influencing contemporary understandings of drug misuse (Gossop, 2007). Images of the 'addict' as emaciated, unkempt, anomic and surrounded by drug paraphernalia such as syringes and needles conjure up tales of moral and physical degradation which locate the drug user as deviant and alien. The book *The Traffic in Narcotics* by Henry J. Anslinger, former US Commissioner of Narcotics, published in 1953, quoted the words of the Supreme Court of the US: 'To be a confirmed drug user is to be one of the walking dead . . . The teeth have rotted out, the appetite is lost, and the stomach and intestine don't function properly' (cited in Gossop, 2007: 181).[2] Whilst such an image seems far-fetched in the twenty-first century, vestiges of this stereotype are still clearly discernible in much of the current discourse relating to drug use and the image of the emaciated addict remains a mainstream element of health promotion to discourage young people from taking drugs. For example, the parents of Rachel Whitear, a British student who died following a heroin overdose, gave permission for disturbing pictures of her drug-wrecked body to form part of a video shown in secondary schools, along with images of her as a 'normal' healthy girl, to promote the message that drug addiction could lead anyone on a journey towards degradation and death.

The stereotypical 'junkie' is far removed from the lived experience of the majority of drug misusers. Many of those in contact with drug treatment agencies, for example, are not involved in crime, may have regular employment, remain in reasonable physical health and are able to control their drug use and maintain a relatively stable lifestyle (Gossop, 2007). According to a heroin user living in North West England in the 1980s:

> It's got a bad stigma to it and that's what's the main problem with it, y'know, this junkie in a dirty squat with a needle hanging out of his arm and OD'ing [overdosing] and dealing on his doorstep and everything and looking like the pictures you see of people falling to bits, but for me personally it's not like that, y'know, I do try to conduct a normal law-abiding life.
>
> (cited in Parker, Bakx and Newcombe, 1988: 86)

Why then is the 'junkie' myth so durable? It is partly due to the double (in some cases multiple) stigma whereby substance use is linked to a number of other deviant behaviours and groups. Compared with the general population, a higher proportion of substance misusers do have a criminal record and are more likely to be unemployed, experience mental illness and come from deprived backgrounds. Drug use is also illegal and the drug user is therefore engaging in an illegal activity. As with the double stigma of HIV, drug misuse is a condition that signals association with a number of other stigmatized statuses. The potential for stigmatization and the associated loss of opportunities is thus multiplied.

The 'junkie' stereotype is associated with drug rather than alcohol misuse. Attitudes toward heavy alcohol use are much more ambivalent as drinking is neither illegal nor in many contexts socially unacceptable. However, when alcohol use leads to disruptive or inappropriate behaviour that affects the ability to fulfil one's role or leads to legal, social or interpersonal problems, then the user becomes labelled 'an alcoholic', and is generally socially reviled.

The symbolism surrounding drug and alcohol misuse serves to reinforce stigma and marginalization. Whereas those that view substance misuse as an illness focus upon the negative impact of such stigma upon the stigmatized, those who are more interested in social control focus upon containment (Room, 2005). The rationale is that as drug misuse is a crime it is right that it should be a stigmatized activity. As a result a number of campaigns have attempted to separate the behaviour from the person. In the words of the Royal College of Psychiatrists' (2003) 'Changing Minds' campaign, 'substance misuse behaviour is stigmatized correctly, whilst the substance misusing individual should have his/her stigma removed to reduce barriers to coming forward for increasingly effective treatment'.

Blameworthy behaviour

Not only is substance misuse associated with deviance but, because it is categorized within the realm of individual choice, substance misusers are held to be responsible for their condition. The deviance of substance misuse is thus underpinned by assumptions of agency and free will. Indeed many categorize it as outside the realm of a medical problem and more related to lifestyle choice. Substance misusers have chosen their lifestyle, disaffiliating from society at large while affiliating with their substance-misusing associates to form what is often referred to as a 'demi-monde' or 'sub-culture'.

Substance misusers are perceived as blameworthy and are thus tarnished with a moral stigma. In a study comparing attitudes towards substance misusers with attitudes towards people with psychiatric disorders, the former were rated more negatively (Link, Phelan, Bresnahan, Stueve and Pescosolido, 1999).

Attitudes towards alcohol use tend to be more ambivalent than towards illicit drug use, reflecting the contradictory relationship that societies have towards alcohol, particularly those where it is used as a mainstream social lubricant. A social attitudes survey in Scotland reveals that 64 per cent of respondents agree that 'Drinking is a major part of the Scottish way of life' and 34 per cent of current drinkers classify not drinking altogether as 'odd'. However, alcohol misuse is widely perceived as troublesome with 46 per cent thinking that it causes more harm than other drugs to Scotland and only 18 per cent agreeing that 'Getting drunk at the weekends is a perfectly acceptable thing to do' (Bromley, Ormston and Scottish Executive Social Research Substance Misuse Research Programme, 2005).

This ambivalence is reflected in attitudes towards people who misuse alcohol. The report notes that:

> People in Scotland are divided over whether problem drinkers can be held 'morally responsible' for their own situation. While 34 per cent agree or strongly agree that people with drinking problems have only themselves to blame, 40 per cent disagree.
>
> (Bromley *et al.*, 2005: 1)

In some ways the 'problem drinker' is more difficult for people to categorize than the drug user as many people enjoy a drink and may drink regularly, making it a challenge to delineate between 'us' (social drinkers) and 'them' (problem drinkers).

'Dangerous individuals'

In general, the substance misuser represents the 'archetypal deviant' living on the fringes of 'normal' cultures and control and is the perfect scapegoat around which society can, and does, unite in condemnation as a form of social control (South, 1999). According to Jock Young (1999: 113), 'Every folk devil sharpens the image of the normal person in the street: in these instances the normal family and the "normal" non-drug user (ignoring the whiskey, strong lager, gin and tonic, cigarettes, barbiturates, Valium, Prozac, beta-blockers, etc, etc!)'. Socially constructed concepts of dangerousness are central to the operation of social categories based on differentiation between the self as 'us' and the other as 'them'. As we have seen in previous chapters, the 'us' and 'them' mentality that underpins stigma involves delineation of boundaries between safety (us) and danger (them). This has long been reflected in the characterization of drug misusers as coming from poor and excluded members of the 'dangerous classes', or more recently 'the underclass'.

The social construction of the 'dangerous individual' is linked to the emergence of the 'sciences' of psychiatry and criminology (Cohen, 1985). Foucault's analysis illustrated how the 'psychiatric gaze' became integrated with the surveillance and treatment of the insane and criminals (Foucault, 1978; Foucault, 1988). The construction of the 'dangerous individual' provided the leverage for psychiatry to penetrate criminology, and as a consequence punishment shifted from the body of the prisoner to the mind (Mason and Mercer, 1999). As the 'psychiatrization of criminal danger' (Foucault, 1978) gained ascendancy, the 'psychiatric gaze' fell not only upon perpetrators of major criminal acts but also upon those committing more minor indiscretions, so that the 'dangerous individual' became an ever expanding category. With the pathologization of offending behaviour there was a shift in focus from the criminal act to the author of the act, the 'dangerous individual'. In Foucault's interpretation the deviance associated with the 'dangerous individual' is based not on the behaviour but upon 'what he is by nature, according to his constitution, character traits or his pathological variables' (Foucault, 1978: 17–18).

Contemporary culture and tabloid journalism in particular capitalize upon and further perpetuate the public horror and fear associated with the 'dangerous individual'. This collective fear of crime and the obsession with pathological deviance has led to the 'dangerous individual' becoming the personification of madness, badness and evil. A focus upon how the 'dangerous individual' responds to their notoriety and maintains a sense of self-identity thus provides a useful exemplar of the personal challenge to a stigmatized status.

The 26 substance misusers whose narratives are discussed below had varied social characteristics and included 20 males and six females aged from 20 to 49, who were mainly unemployed, with 15 in prison at time of interview. All had committed offences and were in contact with the criminal justice system. Although two were serving long sentences for murder the majority had been convicted of minor offences and alternated their time between prison and the community. All but seven of the respondents had mental health problems, including two who were classified as having severe and enduring mental illness. The majority, however, were diagnosed as having either relatively minor or untreatable mental health problems, such as mild depression or personality disorder, and were not eligible for mainstream mental health services, except in times of crisis. Further details of the sample and methods are available elsewhere (Green *et al.*, 2006). Taken as a whole, the sample very much conformed to the stereotype of the 'dangerous individual' and showed full awareness of negative societal attitudes towards them:

> I've had people prejudice [*sic*] against me since I can't remember. They're prejudiced because you're a criminal, because you're a drug addict, they think you're horrible. They can't bear having you around. They try and block you out. Don't want to talk to you. You being there is like a fly irritating them – they're always trying to get rid of you [flicks his hand very sharply as though trying to shoo a fly away from round his face]. They're all prejudiced . . . People just don't understand and what's more don't want to know. They live in their own little world and people like me threaten their little bubble.
>
> (Lee,[3] a male drug user living in the community cited in Green *et al.*, 2006: 311)

Lee is aware of his 'dangerous' social standing and the reference to 'people like me threatening their little bubble' shows he clearly identifies himself as being categorized as the 'other'.

The personal challenge[4]

Being a 'dangerous individual': 'not my fault' narratives

As noted above, there was a generalized awareness amongst respondents in our study that society viewed them as 'other' and potentially dangerous. Their narratives, however, challenged this stigmatized status and suggested that viewing them pejoratively was neither justified nor accurate. They constructed elaborate arguments to show that their ascribed identities as "dangerous individuals" were essentially undeserved.

In the narratives, respondents drew upon features of their background and environment to explain their substance misuse and deviant lifestyle in order to negate personal responsibility for their behaviour. These concepts are elaborated below in what I term 'not my fault' narratives. These included feelings of not being in control of their own destiny and blaming the failings of others to explain irresponsible and/or dangerous aspects of their own behaviours.

'Out of control'

The narratives portrayed lives composed of an ongoing cycle of substance misuse, offending, homelessness and institutionalization over which the respondents had little control. This cycle is eloquently elaborated in the following quote from Shane, a male drug user, which illustrates how the absence of accommodation or money can leave the substance misuser with little choice but to return to a drug-using lifestyle on release from custody:

> What happened was . . . I just walked out of Crown Court, I looked up at the sky, I thought I've got nowhere to live, no money in my pocket, nothing, they just let me out. I'd done four and a half months in prison, so I've absolutely got nothing. And I looked up at the sky and I thought 'here we go again'. I just thought there's nothing I can do really. I can't find accommodation just like that, and I went straight away and rang up one of my friends to ask if I could stay round there. They were selling drugs at the time, and that was it, straight back into it. I knew what was going to happen, because I've experienced that before, coming out of prison etc. I wasn't even prepared to even try because I knew where it ends or whatever, and in the end I just went straight at it. Like bang into it, straight away, which I really don't want to happen this time. But I can see it happening if I haven't got the accommodation.
>
> (cited in Green *et al.*, 2006: 312)

Another respondent, Ed, told a similar tale about the failure of others to provide appropriate support that resulted in a continuous ride on the 'Merry-Go-Round' of the criminal justice system, saying:

> And basically you know, you'd just become, you know, I became the system, I was the process. You know. I was just there, police station, court, remand, sentencing, back out, police station, court, remand sentencing. It's just a Merry-Go-Round, and no-one really wanted to pull me off it.
>
> (cited in Green *et al.*, 2006: 313)

The observation from Ed that he 'became the system, I was the process' was symptomatic of the powerlessness voiced by a number of the respondents. The 'out of control' narratives emphasized the process through which their addiction had unexpectedly 'taken over' their life and the concomitant sense of hopelessness, chaos and above all inability to change lifestyle due to lack of material, social or emotional resources. There were, however, some exceptions such as Colin, who alternated between a life of relative sobriety with his wife and children and one of heroin dependence and eviction from his home by his partner that resulted in his sleeping on the streets or at a homeless shelter. Another respondent, Katy, a 20-year-old female, was determined to change on release from prison despite a history of 12 short periods of incarceration, and had procured both suitable accommodation and an appointment with a counsellor on her release. All of those attempting or thinking about changing their lifestyle in this manner recognized the need for accepting rather than denying responsibility for their former actions. In general, however, denial of responsibility, being 'out of control' and lacking alternatives were central pillars of the narrative frameworks of those who continued as substance misusers.

'Sad tales'

The accounts contained a large number of what Lyman and Scott (1970: 122) called 'sad tales': those that highlight a dismal past to 'explain' an individual's current state. Respondents explicitly drew upon elements of their background, including childhood experiences, to explain their behaviour. John, a young man in his early twenties, felt his substance misuse was related to maltreatment from his parents; he told the interviewer that he did not want to talk about this as 'they [his parents] are only round the corner. If they thought I'd been talking about them, they'd start hitting me again and that'. Narratives alluded to time spent in children's homes, special residential schools or young offenders institutions, often with harsh regimes. They drew upon their unhappiness and isolation in their past to explain their subsequent violent or substance-misusing behaviour.

The link with unhappy and/or abusive episodes in childhood was so much taken for granted that those who had had a relatively problem-free childhood referred to this as something of a mystery. For example, Steve, a male drug user, talked about his childhood and subsequent errant lifestyle with some puzzlement, saying:

> I don't know, I was just a little fucker I suppose. I don't know. Don't know. Because there was nothing wrong in the family or nothing like that, it weren't as though – you know some kids had problems and all that, you know step-dad's [sic] and that – but I didn't have nothing like that, you know I had a good family. My family were good.
>
> (cited in Green *et al.*, 2006: 314–15)

His willingness to accept responsibility for his behaviour was, however, atypical. The respondents much more commonly drew upon 'sad tales' rather than personal choice to explain and 'excuse' their 'deviant' behaviour.

Lack of understanding

Whereas abusive backgrounds were used to justify the onset of substance misuse, inadequate support, particularly from care services, was cited as responsible for respondents' subsequent failure to reform their lifestyle. The 'red tape', that is the bureaucratic procedures that involved appointments and long waits to see someone, was criticized as unsuited to the chaotic nature of the lives of many respondents and was therefore felt to be responsible for their failure to engage positively with services. Such shifting of the blame onto the perceived failings of others was a feature of the 'not my fault' narratives.

Service providers were also criticized for lacking empathy and, although respondents acknowledged that service providers sometimes tried to help, such efforts were frequently dismissed on the grounds that it was impossible for someone who had not experienced substance misuse and social exclusion to 'understand'. Other substance misusers were the only people who would be able to empathize. As Brian, a drug user, said:

> [P]eople here [a drug treatment centre] are all in the same boat. They know where you are coming from. Sometimes I'll have a walk around with another client and a chat and that's helpful. They have had the same experiences as you. They know where you are coming from. They are not reading it out of a textbook.

This shared understanding with other substance users was highly valued along with the notion that they would be non-judgemental. In contrast many care workers were portrayed as lacking empathy and understanding and as being too judgemental. According to Stacey, a female alcohol user:

> I don't like talking to psychiatrists, they box you in, I mean they categorize you too quickly, and if they can't find a category to plonk you in they push you to one side and call you a Borderline Personality Disorder. They just box you in.

She resented being labelled as 'crazy' when in her own eyes she was just 'very very drunk'.

The 'not my fault' narratives thus portrayed 'out of control' lifestyles that emerged as a result of abusive backgrounds and were sustained by the failure of society to provide appropriate support. Their substance-misusing lifestyle was a product of the failure(s) of others rather than the self and their status as 'dangerous individuals' was thus neither of their own making nor, as is shown below, an indication of their 'true selves'.

Construction of the moral self: 'good at heart' narratives

The 'not my fault' narratives which respondents used to negate responsibility for antisocial behaviour were generally accompanied by their claims to be essentially moral and good. These 'good at heart' narratives stressed the 'goodness' of the 'real self' as responsive and responsible in a number of life domains.

The responsive client

In contrast to the 'not my fault' narratives that focused upon the failings of services and service providers, the 'good at heart' narratives stressed the

service support, lack of resources) which unleashed the 'other' within them. They were keen to disassociate this 'other' from their 'true selves'. Through the mechanism of categorizing their irresponsible behaviour as 'other' (i.e. not within their control) and their expressed disapproval of this 'other', they constructed a good and moral true self.

Identity: the moral self

The substance misusers we interviewed (with two exceptions) repudiated their ascribed 'dangerous' label and actively constructed a narrative with a moral framework to demonstrate that they were morally good. In 'not my fault' narratives their behaviour that was censured by society was attributed to the failings of others rather than the self. The 'good at heart' narratives served to illustrate that they were essentially moral and responsible and conformed to the same moral code as others.

By positioning themselves as 'regular' or 'normal' and morally correct, these so-called 'dangerous individuals' distance themselves from the Foucauldian interpretation of the 'dangerous individual' as morally deviant 'by nature' (Foucault 1978: 17–18). In Foucauldian analysis, the dangerous individual is seen as a subject buffeted by elaborate systems and labels of discipline and control. A focus on the narratives of these individuals, however, reveals a more active role in which they sustain a personal challenge and assert moral agency against their ascribed stigmatized label.

This enables them to retain or even reclaim their moral self and their citizenship. However, the impact of this challenge was not sufficient to counteract entirely the negative self-identity associated with substance misuse. The substance misusers we interviewed still reported feeling different from 'normal people', and were also fatalistic about their stigmatized status, feeling trapped by it. One male drug user, Colin, said, 'it's like you are on a boat and you sink and you come up again and then the boat capsizes.' He could not see how to stay afloat, saying 'If I'm a junkie I'm a junkie', and although he talked about plans to lead a normal life and go to college he felt that in reality 'I'm kidding myself here. I'm not going to college.' Although participants reported being keen to 'get a normal life back' they could not quite envisage how this might come about. As Lee put it, 'Everything's in the future, it's like a hologram, it's there but it's not. Like the proverbial rock that as you walk towards it, moves further away.' A sense of hopelessness about the future was evident in the narratives. The personal challenge protected self-identity to some extent but in none of the narratives was the internalization and self-stigma associated with substance misuse and leading to a sense of unworthiness, low self-esteem and loss of hope entirely absent.

Discrimination and exclusion

Although the personal challenge enables the substance misuser to, in the main, protect their sense of selfhood at least to a degree, it is debatable whether it has had any impact on the social exclusion associated with substance misuse. The personal challenge may make them feel better about themselves but there is little evidence that it has an impact upon the attitudes or behaviours of others towards them.

Negative judgements towards substance misusers remain prevalent and are frequently reported in mental health care settings (Rasinski, Woll and Cooke, 2005). A central principle of current guidelines in England is that 'Drug misusers have the same entitlement as other patients to the services provided by the National Health Service' (Department of Health, 2007b: 11), but this is often not sustained in practice. Treatment is offered in a range of health and social care settings and care workers in many non-specialist drug or alcohol services, who share mainstream societal values about the dangerousness of substance misusers, may well hold pejorative views towards them and treat them as stereotypical 'junkies'. This makes treatment more difficult to access (one participant reported being rejected by four general practitioners) and deters substance users from seeking treatment (Parker *et al.*, 1988).

Stigmatization can also hinder recovery and have a longer-lasting effect than the health consequences of substance misuse. A study of people with a dual diagnosis of substance misuse and mental illness found at one-year follow-up that, whereas psychiatric symptoms had largely resolved and drug-taking had mainly stopped, the stigma associated with the condition continued and was associated with high levels of depression (Link *et al.*, 1997). A study of illicit drug users conducted in the US showed that discrimination and alienation were both associated with poorer mental health (Ahern, Stuber and Galea, 2007).

The strong and enduring association between substance misuse and social exclusion remains. People from more deprived backgrounds are more likely to become substance misusers. Abusive backgrounds, disengagement with schooling and behavioural problems sometimes leading to early contact with the criminal justice system during childhood are risk factors for developing a substance-misusing career. Heroin use has been described as 'a "spectre" which hangs over a predominantly deprived urban "underclass" of unqualified, unskilled and unemployed young adults' (Parker *et al.*, 1988: 67). This association is reinforced through substance misuse, which may lead directly to social exclusion in a number of domains such as housing, employment and social relationships. For example, a drug-using female respondent in our study, Katy, reported how she was evicted from her house as it had become a central meeting place for drug users. Having been evicted she was unable to get credible references to obtain alternative housing and she therefore stayed with (drug-using) friends or at a shelter for the homeless. Either of these latter alternatives was a problem as in these settings it was difficult to avoid other drug users and access to drugs.

Substance misusers can also experience difficulties finding and retaining employment. Potential employers may be unwilling to employ people with a criminal record. Furthermore substance misuse is a major cause of losing a job on account of lateness, absenteeism or theft (to finance their habit) (Parker *et al.*, 1988).

Prolonged misuse has a negative and sometimes irreversible impact on social relationships. Substance misuse is one of the principal reasons for children being taken into care (Child Welfare League of America, 2001). Just in the small sample we interviewed many of the fathers had lost all contact with their children, and mothers had children who were in care or adopted as a result of their inability to care for them due primarily to their substance misuse. There is a clear impact on the family with social, emotional and health costs for the drug misusers' children, parents, grandparents and siblings (Barnard, 2007; Parker *et al.*, 1988). For many the cost of supporting a substance-misusing family member is too high and in the words of Colin, a respondent in our study, 'People give up on you. You've got no friends or family.'

The same young man also alludes to the vicious circle of substance misuse and social exclusion, explaining that the latter, which involves sleeping rough and being shunned by family, invariably leads him towards further drug use to feel 'normal' again:

> But I've slept everywhere . . . I've slept in the High Street, I've slept in Mind [an organization offering support to mental health service users] garden, underneath those benches, loads of times. Then I do the gear coz I'm homeless. It brings you back to life, helps you with the pain, you can walk round the street like you were normal.

The evidence would thus suggest that the personal challenge has little impact upon the social exclusion that so often accompanies substance misuse.

Has the stigma associated with substance misuse been reduced?

The personal challenge to stigma for substance misusers involves the construction of narratives refuting the stigmatized label of being a dangerous individual and putting forward a true self who is moral and responsible. Some of the defining features of the personal challenge were identified many decades ago in the literature about delinquency and 'deviance disavowal' discussed above. Thus to what extent can the personal challenge be regarded as contemporary?

One change that is clearly discernible is the increasing normalization of substance misuse and the emergence of a number of positive images associated with substance misusers. Substance misuse and the 'culture of intoxication' have become more ubiquitous in society and it is an increasingly normalized activity (Measham and Brain, 2005; Parker, 2005). There is evidence that alcohol marketing practices, such as the introduction of alcopops, commodify youth identities such that underage drinking is naturalized, normalized and even encouraged (McCreanor, Moewaka Barnes, Gregory, Kaiwai and Borell, 2005).

There are indicators of wider cultural acceptance of recreational drug use in the UK in films and the media as well as greater understanding of the grey area between recreational use and misuse, and the ease with which the former can become the latter. The central character of a current comedy series on national television is Moz, a small-time cannabis dealer who sees himself as providing a crucial service to the community. According to Johnny Vegas, the actor who plays Moz, 'I think Moz is a dealer who has a bit of a conscience really.' (BBC Press Office, 2004).

The excessive behaviour of young celebrities associated with substance misuse (musicians such as Amy Winehouse, Pete Doherty and Britney Spears, and actors such as Lindsay Lohan) generally attracts social opprobrium and images of them leaving nightclubs in an intoxicated state are typically accompanied by negative headlines. One can, however, at the same time detect a normalization of substance misuse associated with creativity and a celebrity lifestyle. In this manner there are positive associations between young celebrities and substance misuse – and the 'cool' factor can enhance celebrity status. For example, the model Kate Moss was photographed snorting cocaine and the images were accompanied with commentary suggesting that her career would be over as a result. In reality quite the reverse happened and she obtained more contracts than ever before, culminating in her being invited to design a clothing range for an apparently respectable high-street chain selling clothes to teenagers and young women.

There is also evidence that young people emulate these style icons. Popular internet sites such as YouTube and social networking sites such as Facebook allow audiences to access and share footage of celebrities or indeed themselves in a state of drunken excess. One young woman interviewed in a popular magazine talked about how she always made sure that her friends photographed her when completely intoxicated so she could post the images on the internet (see *Closer*, 2007). Whereas such behaviour seems bizarre to older generations, it is noteworthy that a Danish study found that teenagers who report high alcohol consumption are regarded most highly by their peers (Demant and Jarvinen, 2006).

Such behaviour, however, seems far removed from the roots of the personal challenge discussed in Chapter 3. To what extent is the young woman posting images of herself on the internet or the substance misusers proclaiming their commitment to mainstream morality connected with those people diagnosed with a long-term condition who struggle to retain their personal identity? To an extent all are products of the more fluid post-modern reflexive identity discussed earlier, the first by glamorizing the moral defectiveness associated with substance misuse, the last two groups by challenging the stigmatizing view of their condition and by their appeals to 'see the person' under the surface. Indeed one of the drug users we interviewed voiced the view that he had found one care worker helpful as he 'Saw the person rather than the disease'. This reclamation of the self whilst withstanding the ravages of a long-term condition is a common feature of the experience of illness in contemporary society.

The narratives of the substance misusers discussed in this chapter are clear examples of the process that Beck (1992) describes as 'reflexive biography', whereby self-reflection and critique are used to define self-identity. This phenomenon is of course one of the hallmarks of the theory of postmodernism. In the example presented in this chapter, substance misusers draw upon their past and often abusive backgrounds to explain who they are and 'excuse' their misdemeanours. They also provide evidence to disassociate their antisocial behaviour from their true selves. Their narratives thus 'reconstitute and repair ruptures between body, self, and world by linking and interpreting different aspects of biography in order to realign present and past and self and society' (Williams, 1984: 197). This process also occurs among those with other conditions. The biographical reconstruction of people with haemophilia and gay men following infection with HIV works to reinforce 'components of their identity that, prior to HIV-infection, had been built around haemophilia or homosexuality' (Carricaburu and Pierret, 1995: 65).

The personal challenge is empowering in that it enables people living with long-term illness to assert some control over their condition and their lives even though the condition itself, or the behaviour associated with it, remains highly stigmatized. The narrative device is integral to the personal challenge and enables a reclamation of moral character and virtue despite having a stigmatized condition. The personal challenge has thus been increasingly influential in combating stigma and has also been one of the driving forces underpinning the organizational challenge discussed in the next chapter.

6 The organizational challenge to stigma

Mental health service users 'reclaim Bedlam'

Mental illness has been described as 'the ultimate stigma' (Falk, 2001), a 'mark of shame' (Hinshaw, 2007). Such designations are increasingly challenged by groups such as Reclaim Bedlam, a service-user[1] organization set up in 1997 to protest against the 750th anniversary celebrations of the Bedlam site organized by the Maudsley NHS Trust. It is one of the many groups that constitute the organizational challenge to stigma in the field of mental health, which is the focus of this chapter.

The chapter begins by examining attitudes towards mental health service users and the nature of the stigma associated with mental illness and then examines the organizational challenge to this stigma. The organizational challenge is complex, multidimensional and diffuse. It operates across a range of levels – local, national and international – involving both service users and service providers. It ranges from a global 'Program Against Stigma and Discrimination' run by the World Psychiatric Association to small-scale local initiatives run by groups of service users. Some challenges have overt social policy objectives whereas others have the more general goal of changing culture and transforming attitudes. In this chapter the theoretical models underlying these initiatives are explored and the tactics that are used are reviewed. The focus of the chapter then shifts to the impact of the organizational challenge upon the stigma associated with mental illness by examining the effect that legislation, anti-stigma campaigns, protest, education and contact have had upon attitudes towards mental illness and the experience of mental health service users.

The chapter draws upon data collected from a study I conducted (with service providers and a mental health advocacy service) between 2000 and 2001 in which we carried out in-depth interviews with mental health service users.[2] The study explored the composition and nature of respondents' social relationships and their experience of marginalization, stigma and discrimination. These data have been analysed to understand the association between social contact and mental health (Green *et al.*, 2002) and to deconstruct respondents' attitudes towards stigma (Green *et al.*, 2003), and this chapter draws upon these findings.

Mental illness: the ultimate stigma?

Prejudicial views and the desire for social distance

In 1998 Norman Sartorius, who was at that time president of the World Psychiatric Association, wrote, 'Stigma and discrimination are the most significant obstacles to the development of mental health care and to ensuring a quality of life to people suffering from mental illness' (Sartorius, 1998: 1058). This assertion is supported by first-hand accounts from those who have experienced mental illness. Kay Redfield Jamison, a psychologist who has suffered from manic depression since the age of 16, stated, 'It would be hard to overstate the degree of stigmatization faced by those who have mental illness: it is pervasive in society, rampant in the media, and common within the medical profession' (Jamison, 1998: 1053). Esso Leete, a mental health service user who has experienced a number of diagnoses (mostly variants of schizophrenia), 15 hospitalizations and 20 medications including electroconvulsive therapy (ECT), concludes that 'there is nothing more devastating, discrediting and disabling to an individual recovering from mental illness than stigma' (cited in Hinshaw, 2007: 129). Leete (1987) documented the discrimination she encountered, which included treatment without consultation, rejection from the college where she was studying, denial of a driving licence, loss of friends, problems finding housing and low expectations by mental health care professionals.

As well as personal accounts, surveys investigating the experiences and the perceptions of mental health service users suggest that stigma is a major obstacle. A survey by Mind (2001), the leading mental health charity in England and Wales, found that 62 per cent of respondents who felt recovered, or were coping with their mental illness, said the main barrier to recovery was the attitude of the general public. A survey of over 1000 mental health service users in the US revealed widespread experience of stigma from communities, families, churches, colleagues and mental health professionals (Wahl, 1999).

There are a plethora of studies showing that socially stigmatizing attitudes towards people with mental health problems are indeed widespread (see for example Byrne, 1997; Byrne, 2001).[3] Prejudicial attitudes are more common among those who are older and with lower educational qualifications (Brockington, Hall, Levings, and Murphy, 1993; Wolff, 1997). In the US, ethnicity has been linked with attitudes towards the mentally ill with those from ethnic minority groups holding more liberal attitudes (Corrigan *et al.*, 2001b). It is suggested that people from so called 'out-groups' who are more likely to have experienced prejudice themselves are less likely to be prejudicial toward others (Fiske 1998).

There is also evidence that attitudes are linked to familiarity with mental illness; those who have more contact with mental health service users are less likely to hold prejudicial attitudes towards them (Corrigan *et al.*, 2001b).

Stigma is, however, rife among the medical profession. A survey in London in 2002 found that one-half of medical students and physicians surveyed thought people with mental illness were dangerous and unpredictable and a recent report from Switzerland suggests psychiatrists are just as likely as the general population to desire social distance from people with schizophrenia (cited in Hinshaw, 2007: 111).

To portray attitudes towards mental health service users as wholly prejudicial, however, would be misleading as public attitudes are largely characterized by ambivalence. Prejudicial attitudes to mental illness have been linked to two constructs: 'authoritarianism' (a belief that people with mental illness require coercive handling) and 'benevolence' (a belief that they should be cared for sympathetically) (Cohen and Struening, 1962). Many people hold broadly benevolent attitudes and, particularly with the advent of community care for those with severe and long-standing mental health problems, recognize their responsibility to provide an inclusive community environment (Brockington *et al.*, 1993; Wolff, 1997).

However, these broadly positive attitudes may not reflect behaviour and both authoritarian and benevolent beliefs are associated with a desire for social distance from mental health service users (Corrigan *et al.*, 2001b). A survey of the general population in the US found that 'a strong stereotype of dangerousness and desire for social distance persist' (Link *et al.*, 1999: 1328).[4] Although many believe that people with mental illness should be treated sympathetically and inclusively there are clear limits to this benevolence and it is rarely translated into desire for close contact (see for example Hall, Brockington, Levings and Murphy, 1993). Mental health service users are perceived to be hard to talk to (Crisp, Gelder, Rix, Meltzer and Rowlands, 2000) and the British Social Attitude survey of the general population reports that only 29 per cent of respondents say that they would feel comfortable if someone with schizophrenia moved in next door and only 19 per cent would feel comfortable with a close relative marrying someone with schizophrenia (Rigg, 2007).

Schizophrenia is perhaps the most stigmatized mental disorder as sufferers are widely perceived as unpredictable, dangerous, aggressive and lacking self-control and most people would not wish to have a close social relationship with them such as sharing a flat (Schulze and Angermeyer, 2003). In a recent survey in Britain (Crisp *et al.*, 2000), respondents perceived that people with schizophrenia, alcoholism and drug addiction were much more likely to be unpredictable and dangerous than those with other types of mental health problem.

Unpredictability and dangerousness

A desire for social distance from mental health service users stems from the perception of unpredictable behaviour associated with mental health problems. The symptoms of some mental disorders can be disturbing and may result in behaviours that threaten social order (Hinshaw, 2007). It has been suggested that people with mental health problems challenge 'the very basis on which American civilization rests' (Falk, 2001: 41). In other words, the danger is as much 'symbolic' as 'real'.

A recent review of the epidemiological literature about the association between mental illness and dangerousness found evidence of a *weak* link between the two which is in contrast to the public perception of a *strong* link between them (Corrigan and Cooper, 2005). An overemphasis upon dangerousness perpetuates discrimination and stigmatizing attitudes and masks the fact that the great majority of mental health service users pose no danger to others. Indeed, they pose a much greater risk to themselves than to others (Ryan, 1998). This, however, has not deterred public health policy makers from prioritizing public safety by way of draconian measures to contain mental health service users who are perceived to be a risk to others (Sayce, 2000).

Notions of dangerousness are fuelled by media coverage of mental illness. Media portrayals of crimes committed by mental health service users have a tendency to sensationalize and promote the view that the mentally ill are violent and dangerous (Angermeyer and Matschinger, 1996; Wolff, 1997). Content analysis of media coverage about mental illness showed that violence to others received most coverage and easily outnumbered more sympathetic images (Philo *et al.*, 1994). Focus groups with audiences confirmed the strong influence of media accounts on their attitudes (ibid.). There is also evidence from the US that media representation of mental illness in the 1950s emphasized the more bizarre symptoms (Nunnally, 1961).

Among mental health researchers there has been much debate and research about the relative impact and relationship between aberrant behaviour, labelling and stigma to determine whether it is the behaviour or the label that leads to social rejection (see Chapter 2). A series of studies conducted by Link and colleagues (Link, 1987; Link, Cullen, Frank and Wozniak, 1987; Link and Phelan, 1999) suggested that people with a mental illness label were stigmatized even if their behaviour was 'normal' and led to the construction of 'modified labelling theory' whereby labelling was linked to negative societal reaction and this in turn exacerbated the course of a person's illness. There is clear evidence that, whereas aberrant behaviour on the part of mental health service users is an important source of stigma, the effects of labels reinforce this stigma (Hinshaw, 2007).

It has been noted that much of the evidence on stigma and discrimination towards mental illness is based on attitude surveys and simulated laboratory experiments rather than the lived experience of mental health service users (Schulze and Angermeyer, 2003) so it is to this aspect that we now turn.

Discrimination and exclusion

Forms of discrimination against mental health service users may be 'direct', such as legal restrictions, or 'indirect', such as being refused accommodation or employment as a result of their mental health condition. There is evidence of legal restrictions and structural imbalances built into legal regulations. Currently in about half the states of the US, people with mental illness are restricted from one or more of the following activities: voting, holding office, marriage, child custody, serving on a jury (Hinshaw, 2007). In the UK, many women with severe and enduring mental illness experience problems gaining child custody and in the early twentieth century some were sterilized (Sayce, 2000). It has been suggested that 'discrimination begins inside the mental health system' (Sayce, 2000: 65) in that people may be treated without consent over a long period and the views of service users are often ignored or dismissed. Perhaps the strongest evidence for overt discrimination against mental health service users is that, in countries like the UK, they are the only group in society who can be deprived of their liberty without having done anything wrong and without reference to the criminal justice system.

As part of its 'Respect' campaign, Mind conducted a survey of mental health service users about the stigma and discrimination they had experienced (Read and Baker, 1996). This showed that 47 per cent reported verbal or physical harassment in public, 34 per cent had been dismissed or forced to resign from their work and 24 per cent had been refused insurance or financial services.

Unemployment and discrimination in the workplace is commonplace (Hinshaw, 2007). Another survey conducted by Mind reported that 53 per cent of 516 mental health service users (all of whom had experienced at least one psychiatric hospitalization) were in employment when they first experienced a mental health crisis. By the time of the survey only 20 per cent had a job and only 11 per cent were in full-time employment, leading the researchers to conclude that employment is 'severely and irreversibly damaged by entering the role of psychiatric patient' (Rogers, Pilgrim and Lacey, 1993: 93). The employment level of former psychiatric patients is usually below 10 per cent and those who do have a job work fewer hours for less money (Huxley and Thornicroft, 2003).

High unemployment inevitably leads to high rates of poverty, which can lead to further exclusion as many activities, such as social events, become too costly and there is evidence of downward social drift (Ryan, 1998). One-third of the homeless population in the US have a history of mental illness and others live in poor-standard housing often in marginal neighbourhoods (Hinshaw, 2007).

Even those who have financial resources may face rejection. A woman in Germany whose son had schizophrenia said that she and others wanted to build a supported housing project using their own money but were unable to do so owing to opposition from residents in the area:

> The problem is that we live in one of the most beautiful residential areas, a very posh neighbourhood. There are a lot of celebrities living there, only rich people, all millionaires. And they founded a citizens' initiative, put posters up everywhere saying: 'Psychiatry in our neighbourhood –

never!'. And one of these famous folks, the president of a very popular football club, said at one of their meetings: 'Nobody will build a mad-house in our area! And I will personally take care of that!'

(cited in Schulze and Angermeyer, 2003: 306)

Mental health service users also report stigma and discrimination at an interpersonal level. Close relationships become unbalanced, the parenting role is disrupted, 'friends drift away' and isolation and loneliness are frequently reported (Green *et al.*, 2002). In interviews we conducted with 15 female and 12 male mental health service users, the shrinking of social networks was a common theme. The respondents had a range of mental disorders, mostly a major psychotic or depressive illness which was chronic and had a profound effect on their functioning and biographies.[5] According to Ben,[6] a young man with a long-standing personality disorder who was talking about his lack of social contacts, 'I think they thought, "he's gone downhill. I'm not going to bother with him no more"'; another talked about how all his friends gradually got 'compassion fatigue' and drifted away. This trend has also been noted among service users in Germany (Schulze and Angermeyer, 2003) and a number of studies provide evidence of smaller networks, less social support and even 'network collapse' among mental health service users (Lipton, Cohn, Fischer and Katz, 1981).

In the interviews we conducted, 14 of the 27 respondents reported experiences of overt discrimination from close contacts and from 'people in general'. Doris recalled a neighbour taunting her, 'She was saying "You've been in a mental hospital, in the bin and all this. You should go back there."'

Gracie, a woman in her sixties who had spent most of her life in institutional care, described how her sister's stigmatizing attitude was not confined to her mental state but also spilled over to her physical appearance in that 'she used to say I looked as if I come from that place [residential care] with my hair tied back a lot', thus making Gracie feel that even people on the street would know 'there's something wrong with you' (cited in Green *et al.*, 2003: 227).

Disclosure of mental illness may thus elicit negative and hostile reactions but it would appear that more people report perceived stigma than actual discrimination (Green *et al.*, 2003). This has also been reported among those with obsessive–compulsive disorder (Fennell and Liberato, 2007), and among those with other illnesses such as epilepsy (Jacoby, 1994) and HIV (Green and Sobo, 2000).

Perceived stigma is therefore a major factor in the social exclusion of mental health service users. That is not to say that discrimination has been overstated, but more to draw attention to the impact that fear of stigma and discrimination can have. Mental health service users are likely to hold the same negative views about mental illness as other people. The general perception among our respondents was that having a mental illness marks you out as different and has an impact upon how others relate to you. For this reason, respondents reacted strongly against being labelled with an illness, which was felt to give other people licence to relate to the label rather than the person. According to Jason:

> I'm very wary that people might not take me for what I am you see, and put a label on me. Yes, I, it hurt me quite a bit when I was younger that I had been labelled paranoid schizophrenic . . . Of course I got the same label as people like the Yorkshire Ripper [Peter Sutcliffe, the serial murderer of women in Yorkshire who is currently serving a life sentence], people like that you know which I find quite hurtful really you know and I am very conscious about it.
>
> (cited in Green *et al.*, 2003: 227)

Those who perceive higher levels of discrimination are more likely to apply strategies such as concealment, non-disclosure and social withdrawal in order to avoid negative reactions (Link, Cullen, Struening, Shrout and Dohrenwend, 1989). Fear of stigma encourages secrecy and non-disclosure and the following quote from Jed shows how careful he is not to disclose his mental health status to others:

> Well, if somebody doesn't know I never ever tell them. I never ever speak about it [his mental health] . . . never make any reference to it whatsoever. They'd never know about the mental illness 'cause I'd never tell them . . . I do keep it to me self.
>
> (cited in Green *et al.*, 2003: 228)

And Gordon, who has had mental health problems since childhood, said, 'I sort of more or less struggle to keep up appearances . . . I think that's what I've been doing for as long as I can remember' (cited ibid.). This leads people to avoid situations where it is not possible to pass as 'normal': not applying for jobs that might entail having to disclose their health history; not going out with friends if they feel their illness may be noticeable; not confiding in friends about their health problems. Such concealment is also widely reported elsewhere (see for example Hinshaw, 2007; Schulze and Angermeyer, 2003; Wahl, 1999).

Lowered self-esteem?

Stigma, whether enacted or perceived, may be internalized and a negative valuation of oneself can result in shame and self-loathing (Link and Phelan, 2001). As illustrated in Chapter 2, this is an integral part of the stigmatizing process and has a profound impact on social identity.[7] In our study, even though the majority of respondents were of the opinion that the stigma associated with mental illness was unjustified, they all to some extent internalized it and recognized that it had affected their identity. One respondent, Robert, who had enjoyed a regular student life prior to the onset of his mental health problems, felt he was now 'unworthy' to continue with his former life. He expected 'people normally just to sort of write me off as a dull person' and felt that his former friends were fully justified in 'drifting away' because his mental state had tarnished his personality:

> I think if people don't like mentally ill people that's simply because they're mentally ill that's fair enough because you like somebody or you should like them for their personality and their personality is part of their mental state and you can't say his personality is affected by his mental illness because there is no cut off point. You can't say 'well that's', you know, 'I mean he's affected thus he's allowed to be an unpleasant person' but in terms of his personality you can't really you know. It's quite acceptable for this stigma I think personally.
>
> (cited in Green *et al*., 2003: 229–30)

He portrays his mental illness as an integral part of himself resulting in what he sees as a 'spoiled', defiled identity.

That internalization of stigma damages self-esteem is well documented and a meta-analysis concludes that 'stigma does have an observable association with stigmatized groups' mental health' (Mak, Poon, Pun and Cheung, 2007: 256). However, this association is less strong for people with mental health conditions than for those with physical conditions, perhaps as a result of the difficulty of disentangling the impact of stigma from the impact of mental illness *per se*. In our study, for example, the 'drifting away' of social contacts appeared to be related to both the stigma and the symptoms of mental illness. One woman felt that her boyfriend had ended their relationship as a result of her chronic depression but also revealed how she had spent several weeks in her house with the curtains drawn shunning social contact by not answering the doorbell or the telephone.

It is also clear that not everyone's self-esteem is damaged by stigma, especially among those who question the legitimacy of negative acts and stigma associated with their condition. For example, Camp and colleagues, in interviews with female mental health service users, found that although they accepted that they had mental health problems and were aware of negative societal attitudes they did not accept them as valid and therefore rejected them as applicable to the self (Camp, Finlay and Lyons, 2002).

There are a number of strategies to protect self-esteem from negative societal attitudes. These include attributing negative feedback to the prejudice of others rather than the failing of self and comparing one's own outcomes favourably with other members of one's group (Crocker and Major, 1989). Such strategies are often developed and certainly enhanced through participation in service-user groups. In a model developed by Corrigan and Watson (2002) there are three diverse responses to the impact of stigma: internalization leading to self-stigma; indifference; 'righteous anger'. It is this final response in particular that is at the heart of the organizational challenge to stigma, to which we now turn.

The organizational challenge

Models underlying anti-stigma initiatives

There are a number of theoretical models underpinning antidiscrimination work, and Sayce (2000) identifies the following: the brain disease model; the individual growth model; the libertarian model; and the disability inclusion model. These four models overlap and intersect with other typologies used to describe mental health social movements since the late twentieth century such as the mental hygiene movement, the civil rights movement, the antipsychiatry movement and the 'user' or survivor movement (Crossley, 2006).

The brain disease model is firmly rooted in a biomedical paradigm in that it is based upon the belief that mental illnesses are brain diseases with genetic or biochemical origins. SANE, a mental health charity in the UK, subscribes to the biomedical model. It was established in 1986 in response to a series of articles featured in *The Times* newspaper entitled 'Schizophrenia – The Forgotten Illness' written by Marjorie Wallace, SANE's chief executive. The articles focused upon the neglect of people suffering from schizophrenia and the lack of services and information to support them (Crossley, 2006). SANE places a high priority on research and funds an independent research centre, The Prince of Wales International Centre for SANE Research, which aims to advance understanding of the causes and treatment of schizophrenia and bipolar disorder. Its biomedical focus is illustrated by a recent article on its website discussing the evidence of a genetic basis for a link between left-handedness and a predisposition to psychosis.

A focus on biological causality removes any blame attached to mental illness. However, as we have seen in earlier chapters, the link between health and morality is firmly entrenched in our culture and even though people may rationalize that those who are ill are not morally weak they may intuitively label them as such. The brain disease model has attracted much opposition (in both theory and practice) from the antipsychiatry and survivor movements for diverting attention away from environmental factors and discrimination, and for being paternalistic and thus undermining the notion of mental health service users as responsible citizens (Crossley, 2006; Sayce, 2000).

The second of Sayce's categories is the individual growth model, in which there is a continuum from ill health to emotional well-being. Everyone is somewhere on this 'distress continuum', as even the most healthy individuals experience distress on occasions and everyone would therefore benefit from some kind of therapy. This philosophy underpins the ubiquitous 'problem page' and 'agony aunt' columns in many mainstream magazines. It also underlies the influential Layard Report, in which a group of eminent psychiatrists and other mental health experts recommend increasing access to psychological therapies, especially Cognitive Behavioural Therapy, for a far greater proportion of the UK population than hitherto (Centre for Economic Performance's Mental Health Policy Group, 2006). Although the Layard Report retains an emphasis on those with mental health problems, it nevertheless broadens the category and blurs the distinction between the mentally ill and the rest of society. Campaigns based upon the individual growth model tend to focus on those at the less severe end of the spectrum and stress their 'normalness'. This broadening of definition may lead to destigmatization of minor mental health problems but is unlikely to impact upon the stigma associated with more severe and enduring problems. The approach is also based on individual solutions rather than environmental ones and thus does little to tackle discrimination in society at large (Sayce, 2000).

The libertarian model is summed up as 'Equal civil rights and equal criminal responsibility for mental patients' (Sayce, 2000: 116).[8] The intellectual basis of such assertions is the antipsychiatry movement associated with Thomas Szasz (1974) and others who in the 1960s and 1970s rejected terms such as 'mental illness' and 'mental health problems' on the grounds that these pathologize what they would categorize as strange or deviant behaviour rather than illness. Mental health laws are seen as discriminatory *per se* because they allow the state to exercise control over people who exhibit unusual behaviour by labelling them as having 'mental health problems'. Treatment without consent is seen as oppression and the mental health system in general, and psychiatrists in particular, are depicted as oppressive, hence the term 'psychiatric survivor', which alludes to surviving the system rather than the illness (Campbell, 1992).

In addition to challenging the mental health professions, psychiatric survivors also emphasize the value of the mental illness experience. The organization Mad Pride, which positions itself within the civil rights movement, is an excellent example of the libertarian model. Members of Mad Pride do not seek to disown or downplay their health status but proudly claim their difference (Crossley, 2006). On their website it states, 'Mad Pride is committed to ending discrimination against psychiatric patients, promoting survivor equality and celebrating Mad culture' (Mad Pride, 2008).

The libertarian model has been very influential and has also had an impact upon more mainstream advocacy groups, such as Mind, which have consistently opposed compulsory ECT. Mind recently conducted a survey and publicized the findings about negative side effects related to ECT to influence the political debate about the new Mental Health Bill (Mind, 2008).

The civil liberties perspective has not, however, been without its critics, and has been blamed for the rise in homicides committed by people discharged from psychiatric hospitals and for cuts in mental health services (Sayce, 2000). It has also been noted that service users are keener to demand rights than accept responsibility for their actions and would, for example, expect diversion from a custodial sentence if their mental health state was implicated in criminal activity, although they may reject compulsory mental health treatment.

The fourth model is the disability inclusion model, which has a very broad plural agenda in that it looks towards failings in social systems and covers all domains such as the legal system, medical treatment, media, housing and employment. It is based on the social model of illness discussed in Chapter 2, which locates the problem and the need for change at the societal level. From this perspective, the onus is put on 'society' to ensure that the social environment is non-stigmatizing and socially inclusive for all its citizens.

The disability inclusion model has resulted in numerous alliances of disabled people, although this has not been entirely straightforward because mental health service users have not been universally welcomed by these organizations and they themselves have sometimes resisted being labelled 'disabled'. Coming together around a 'common cause' it would seem is easier in rhetoric than in reality. Nevertheless, alliances of those with long-term conditions have been influential, particularly for example in the movement for independent living.

The distinctions between the different models are by no means always clear-cut and it is possible to detect elements of all of them in the campaigning work of mental health organizations such as Mind. Although there have been intense disagreements between different campaigning groups, their overall contribution to user empowerment has been considerable. The increasingly influential voice of the service user has become a key part of the care landscape.

Tactics of anti-stigma campaigns

Three main strategies have been deployed in order to combat stigmatizing attitudes toward mental illness: protest, education and contact (Corrigan *et al.*, 2001a; Corrigan and Penn, 1999). Protest is used effectively by the contemporary mental health user movement. Crossley (1999) identifies the birth of the movement in the UK as the 1973 formation of the Mental Patients Union, which was a group of patients and staff who came together and led a successful protest against the proposed closure of the Paddington Day Hospital, a therapeutic community in London. From this the idea of a permanent 'union' emerged from which 'mental patients' could proactively campaign and lobby.

There have since been numerous mental health service user organizations challenging the hegemony of the psychiatric profession in particular and stigma and discrimination in society more generally. The establishment of Survivors Speak Out (SSO) in 1986 signalled a new type of service-user activism which revolved around self-advocacy and the desire for people to speak out and act for themselves. The late Peter Shaughnessy, a service user and member of SSO who was also a founder member of Reclaim Bedlam and later Mad Pride, notes in response to setting up the former, 'It was time to take the debate out of the walls of the asylum and into society. Direct action was a springboard to get our undiluted voice out there' (Shaughnessy, 2001: 185). Protest has continued to this day as in the recent action by former residents of a specialist psychiatric hospital, the Henderson Hospital, which saved it from the threat of permanent closure. However, user-led organizations increasingly use a wide range of tactics and many have broadened in scope. Mad Pride, for example, is as much about entertainment, awareness-raising and developing networks as protest (Shaughnessy, 2001).

Anti-stigma and antidiscrimination activities are not confined to those that are user-led but also include campaigns orchestrated by statutory, non-statutory and professional bodies interested in improving the lives of service users. For example, in the UK the Royal College of Psychiatrists and globally the World Psychiatric Association have been very active in promoting anti-stigma initiatives. Such initiatives tend to focus upon education and aim to dispel myths about mental illness and promote more informed and caring attitudes. The Royal College of Psychiatrists initiated two campaigns: 'Defeat Depression' from 1991 to 1996 (Paykel *et al.*, 1997) and 'Changing Minds: Every Family in the Land' from 1998 to 2003 (Crisp, 2000). In the main, these initiatives aim to persuade people who do not have mental health problems to behave in a non-stigmatizing socially inclusive way towards those who do.[9] In general, evaluation of the effectiveness of such projects suggests short-term impact in terms of improved attitudes but the scale and duration of any improvement tends to be very limited (Watson and Corrigan, 2005).

The third strategy involves bringing mental health service users into contact with others in order to challenge the prejudice associated with stereotypes about mental illness. Contact, particularly that which is informal, regular and with institutional support, is effective and this has promoted location of supported housing in community settings and supported employment schemes in mainstream workplaces (Hinshaw, 2007). In the UK, for example, the Department of Health has a programme, SHiFT, that aims to reduce stigma and discrimination directed at service users in the workplace (SHiFT, 2007).

Anti-stigma campaigns often use a combination of the three strategies (protest, education and contact) described above. In the US, a national survey of initiatives aimed at combating stigma and discrimination was assessed by an expert panel composed of health care providers, service users, researchers and educators (Estroff *et al.*, 2004). The panel selected what they considered to be exemplary programmes, which were then analysed to identify key qualities. These included a range of attributes related to language, power, scope, humour, drama, health promotion, benefits for participants as well as audiences, impact and innovation. All the exemplary programmes demonstrated empowerment of and for service users (ibid.).

Legislation has also been used to combat stigma, or more particularly discrimination, and many campaigns target specific legislation. In the UK the Mental Health Alliance, a coalition of 75 organizations including user groups, professional groups, voluntary associations, carer associations and other advocacy groups, works to influence mental health legislation. The Alliance organized widespread protest in the UK against some proposals relating to compulsory treatment and detention. Commenting on new legislation in 2007, the Alliance noted that 'The Government has missed an historic opportunity to achieve a modern and humane new Mental Health Act, but has made important concessions to protect patients and their families from abuse and neglect' (Mental Health Alliance, 2007).

Impact of the organizational challenge

A lot can be gleaned about the impact of the organizational challenge from a brief look at the terminology surrounding mental health service users. As historic categories have been challenged, language has become a political minefield and all terms used have been criticized at some level (Perkins and Repper, 2001). The term 'mental health patient' implies passivity, lack of personal agency and lack of value. More neutral terms such as 'user', 'consumer' or 'client' are felt to imply that the user has a choice whereas in reality many do not as treatment may be coercive. It also, by definition, does not include those who choose not to use services. More radical terms such as 'survivor', coined by those who feel they have 'survived' the trauma of service contact, have been used by those who challenge mainstream psychiatry but not all service users feel the term is appropriate, and even fewer embrace the language of 'mad pride' that celebrates difference. The language of 'distress' has been suggested as a way forward as it 'implies a continuum' (Perkins and Repper, 2001: 152) and is inclusive but it does not acknowledge the reality of difference for many service users.

Have public attitudes changed?

Campaigns and other initiatives targeted at the general population tend to have limited impact and are mostly perceived by their target audience as being irrelevant, boring and unconvincing (Sayce, 2000). There is even some evidence that campaigns that focus on conveying the 'brain disease' theory may lead to higher levels of stigma as a biological or genetic cause may be interpreted as a quality of the person. Campaigns based on a psychosocial model that emphasize environmental stressors such as poverty and unemployment may be more effective (Watson and Corrigan, 2005). However, in general, the evidence for effectiveness is at best mixed (Hinshaw, 2007), and neither public education campaigns nor the increasing integration of psychiatric services in the community have radically altered the stigma associated with mental illness (Phelan and Link, 1998; Phelan, Link, Stueve and Pescosolido, 2000).

A comparison of public conceptions about mental illness in 1950 and 1996 shows that attitudes towards mental illness are broadening over time to include people with non-psychotic disorders but that this has not resulted in a reduction of the perceived threat associated with mental ilness (Phelan *et al.*, 2000). Rather, it would seem that a polarization in attitudes has occurred according to type of mental disorder, with greater acceptance of people with non-psychotic disorders, as these can affect anyone, even 'us', and greater fear of people with psychosis, who remain firmly entrenched in the public perception as 'other' (Phelan *et al.*, 2000). A similar divide was reported about attitudes of young people in England towards people who have mental health problems. Those whose problems were associated with environmental factors such as unemployment or life-events such as bereavement were considered safe and understandable as this could happen to anyone, whereas others were categorized as 'mentally ill' and were perceived to be mysterious, odd and 'other' (Health Education Authority, 1997).

Attitudinal change is more likely in response to contact with mental health service users, particularly if the service users portray non-stereotypical images and if the contact enables opportunities to develop ongoing social relationships (Sayce, 2000). A focused educational campaign took place in an area in which supported houses for mental health service users were located. The campaign was targeted at 150 people living in the neighbourhood and included information, meetings between neighbourhood residents and staff of the supported housing and an invitation to neighbours to social events held in the supported houses to meet further with staff and with the residents themselves. The campaign was successful in reducing the fear of neighbours and a small percentage retained ongoing contact with the supported housing residents. Contact with service users was assessed to be the most effective element of the campaign (Wolff, 1997).

The media can also be a powerful vehicle for shaping attitudes, and mental health service user groups increasingly challenge negative media messages and work with the media to convey more positive images and the reality of living with a mental health problem. One such example is the powerful documentary screened in the UK on national television (BBC2) in September 2006: *Stephen Fry: The Secret Life of the Manic Depressive*. Stephen Fry is a well-known comedian and actor who has bipolar disorder. In the documentary he talks frankly about his own experience of living with this disorder, particularly the mood swings which led to his much publicized disappearance when he walked out of a West End play he was starring in and 'went missing' for a number of days, culminating in a suicide attempt.

Although there is no research evidence that this documentary changed attitudes, it was widely commented upon in the media and was regularly referred to in public discourse. In the two years since the programme was made, Stephen Fry's reputation as an entertainer has continued to grow and his mental health experience has become an integral part of his fame. This is symptomatic and suggestive of widespread cultural acceptance of at least some forms of mental illness in some kind of people. In the past public figures went to great lengths to hide mental health problems whereas the social climate now enables some to 'go public'. Although this is mainly confined to celebrities in the entertainment industry who may feel that their public image is 'enhanced' through public disclosure of mental health vulnerability (which has a long and enduring association with creativity), it is also evident among public figures in other areas of life. John Prescott, the former deputy Prime Minister to Tony Blair (1997–2007), who has a reputation as a robust political bruiser, recently disclosed his struggle with bulimia. And Liz Miller, a general practitioner who has bipolar disorder of sufficient severity to have required compulsory treatment on a number of occasions, co-founded the Doctors' Support Network, which lobbies to raise awareness and provide greater support and understanding from the institutions of the medical profession such as the General Medical Council, which she believes is currently 'medieval in its treatment of mental health problems' (Liz Miller, cited in *The Guardian*, 2008a).

Thus there is some evidence that attitudes towards certain types of mental health problems may be becoming more accepting but also evidence to support the polarization of attitudes whereby the generalized liberalization is accompanied by a more entrenched fear of and desire for social distance from those with overtly psychotic symptoms.

How do education campaigns affect service users?

There is an implicit assumption in many campaigns that education will make general attitudes less stigmatizing and as a result the quality of life of mental health service users will improve. However, research based on the impact of a well-resourced public campaign about leprosy suggests that the impact was detrimental rather than beneficial to people who had the condition (Navon, 1996). The campaign aimed to destigmatize leprosy by focusing on medical advances that meant that leprosy was treatable/curable and to stress the 'normality' of people who had the condition. According to Navon, the main message of the campaign was not internalized as people continued to report stigmatizing attitudes towards people with leprosy, which she attributed to the fact that the image of the socially ostracized indigent leper was far too firmly culturally entrenched and embedded in the spoken language for any campaign to have an impact.[10] In fact, the campaign inadvertently obstructed the stigma management strategies of many people with leprosy who 'did not look like lepers' (Navon, 1996: 266), that is did not conform to the disfigured stereotype and were able to 'pass' as normal. The majority chose to keep their diagnosis secret and thus avoid stigma and lead normal lives. The campaign message, which emphasized the 'normality' of people with leprosy, threatened to 'unmask' them and reveal them to be 'lepers'. In this sense, the education campaign failed to lessen stigma and may have had the opposite effect.

An analysis of the potential impact of destigmatization campaigns on mental health service users suggests similar processes may well be occurring (Green *et al.*, 2003). Campaigns that are intended to combat prejudice by highlighting the prevalence of hostile attitudes may inadvertently contribute to the development of the stigmatized stereotype. Highlighting stigma and blaming others may be a useful coping mechanism for some mental health service users by provoking righteous anger and protecting their self-esteem, but it may have quite the reverse impact on others. For those newly diagnosed and those without the support of other mental health service users, campaigns that highlight the stigma of mental illness may act to reinforce their sense of perceived stigma and 'otherness'. One of the service users we interviewed, Karen, felt that the term 'mental illness' was itself a badge of notoriety. As she put it, 'It's like a stereotype, mental health you know . . . you're an axe murderer or whatever' (cited in Green *et al.*, 2003: 228). Highlighting such stigmatizing stereotypes may exacerbate service users' sense of difference.

The impact of legislation

Legislation clearly has had some impact and in the field of employment the Americans with Disabilities Act (ADA), similar to the Disability Discrimination Act (DDA) in the UK, has had an impact on employers' behaviours but not their attitudes to employing mental health service users (Scheid, 2005). Based on survey responses from 117 employers in a major southern metropolitan area of the US, Scheid concluded that the legislation had not changed employer attitudes:

> If employers do not view those with mental disabilities as employable, or if employers believe that accommodations will be costly or inefficient, they are unlikely to make any meaningful attempt to hire individuals from this traditionally stigmatized group, despite the ADA's provisions to the contrary. Conversely, if employers view the ADA as an important statement of changing social values, or if employers believe that ADA violations will result in heightened litigation risks, they may significantly change their hiring practices, even without concerted enforcement activity.
>
> (Scheid, 2005: 671)

Employers' reasons for complying with ADA are threefold: to avoid a lawsuit; because it is the right thing to do; to ensure everyone has equal rights to employment. The sample in this study was roughly equally split between those who voiced the first, coercive, rationale and those who voiced more inclusive rationales. Over one-half had made adjustments, such as changed work hours, to facilitate the employment of mental health service users. They also voiced concern about the dangerousness of employees with mental health problems due to either the potential for unpredictable behaviour or the side effects of medication, which it was thought might make mental health service users unsuitable for operating certain equipment.

Likewise in the UK a survey commissioned by the Disability Rights Commission in 2007 found that legislation such as the DDA, which was first introduced in 1995 and significantly extended in 2005, and which aims to end discrimination against disabled people, might lead to some changes in practice but may have a limited impact on attitudes. One-third of the small and medium-sized businesses surveyed perceived that mental health problems could affect work performance and potentially pose a health and safety risk (SHiFT, 2007).

Thus legislation may make it somewhat easier for current and past mental health service users to find and/or retain employment, but they may be restricted to less demanding, more routine tasks in the workplace. Legislation on its own is unlikely to be sufficient to achieve cultural change.

A voice and support for the service user

Debates about the effectiveness of anti-stigma campaigns notwithstanding, there is little doubt that the organizational challenge has had a dramatic impact upon service users. Since the 1970s there has been an extraordinary growth of self-help and advocacy movements, which, according to Hinshaw (2007: 222), has

> marked a sea change in the status of people with mental disorders, and particularly their families, from passive, blameworthy, and largely invisible victims to advocates for personal and family well-being, as well as social change.

There is now a wide array of support available to mental health service users and a myriad of organizations offering them opportunities to engage with a variety of diverse activities. For example, at a conference organized by and targeted at mental health service users in south Essex, I collected literature about Good Companions, a befriending service to reduce the isolation of mental health service users and help them to rediscover meaningful social activities; Service Users Network Representation in South Essex (SUNRISE), a network promoting social inclusion of service users; Basildon Eating Disorders and Mental Health Support (BEAMS), a user-led group offering group support and helplines for people with eating disorders; Southend Advocacy Service, offering service users support in making informed decisions and to ensure that their voice is heard; Rethink and Together, both national support groups promoting empowerment among, and improving the quality of life of, service users via campaigns, volunteer networks, information, fund raising and provision of some services; and guidelines for service users and carers entitled 'How can we work together?', produced by a statutory service providing secondary mental health care.

Service users have an active role in all these organizations – many are user-led and even those that were established in the pre-user involvement era now have a clear remit to engage with service users at both strategic and operational levels.[11] The service-user perspective and experience has become highly valued and service users are thus qualified as expert consultants to contribute to the development and shaping of services. This expertise has equipped them with 'a marketable form of cultural capital which they [are] able to use to improve both mental health services and their own circumstances' (Crossley, 2006: 203).

Involvement with self-help, advocacy and campaigning groups is helpful for those taking part and it is claimed that the benefits for service users of participating in anti-stigma campaigning 'can hardly be overestimated' (Estroff *et al.*, 2004: 505). In many of the exemplary programmes identified by Estroff *et al.*, service users worked alongside others from a range of backgrounds and professions and enjoyed relationships on an equal footing.

Being involved and identifying with other mental health service users fosters social support and empowerment, and a growing number of service users are prepared to engage with mental health user groups. Empowerment is generally associated with higher self-esteem and lower levels of shame, and involvement in advocacy helps to empower people to resist stigma when it is encountered. It also encourages service users to attribute stigma to 'external factors' such as the prejudice of others rather than 'internal factors' such as the unworthiness of self. Such an approach is clearly somewhat protective to self-esteem.

However, not all mental health service users engage with service-user groups or seek to form supportive relationships with other service users. Often attitudes towards other service users are ambivalent and many would rather be accepted as 'normal' and mix with 'normal' people (Green *et al.*, 2002). For example, Robert, the service user discussed earlier who felt his mental health problems had turned him into a 'spoiled', unpleasant person, views other mental health users in a similar light, saying 'a lot of the people in my age group who have mental health problems I find obnoxious'. Both Robert and others we interviewed were keen to retain a certain distance between themselves and other service users and, even though they sometimes relied upon them for company at drop-in or treatment centres, made a clear distinction between these contacts and 'really good friends' (Green *et al.*, 2002).

However, of the 27 people we interviewed, two respondents were very active in the self-help movement, and had established strong and enduring links with other mental health service users in a group bonded by mutual support and solidarity. Most of the other respondents, including Robert quoted above, had some contact with other service users in settings other than the delivery of treatment and thus to some degree opted in to the self-help groups and services on offer and felt that this improved the quality of their lives. It would appear that the organizational challenge has had a positive impact on many service users.

To what extent has political action combated the stigma of mental illness?

The organizational challenge to the stigma associated with mental ill health is diverse and multifaceted. The array of activity and organizations that have developed over the last few decades is extraordinary. But to what extent have they succeeded in destigmatizing mental illness?

The move towards care in the community has tackled the segregation of institutional care and aimed to end the dependency culture by emphasizing the rights of mental health service users but, according to Sayce (2000: 82), this and other reforms have 'not tackled discrimination or segregation *per se*' and, 'at present, user/survivors enjoy only the illusion of citizenship' (ibid.: 83).

Stigma is still apparent in the wider cultural milieu. For example, a television critic reviewing a television programme about radical treatment provided to a doctor who hears voices concludes that 'I am sure Ruth [name of doctor featured in the programme] will be an unusually perceptive and empathetic doctor. With a bit of luck, not mine' (*The Guardian*, 2008b).

Yet such attitudes do not go unchallenged. There now exists, for example, a Campaign for the Abolition of the Schizophrenia Label (CASL), an organization that has all the hallmarks of a mental health user movement of the twenty-first century.[12] CASL is a coalition of service-user groups (Hearing Voices Network and supporters of *Asylum* magazine), mental health professionals and academics who draw upon scientific evidence (or in this case what it perceives to be a lack of it) to support its cause. The campaign is driven firstly by questioning the 'science' and usefulness of the schizophrenia diagnosis and secondly in acknowledgement of the damage the label causes to those who have been given this diagnosis. According to their website:

> The desire of our campaign to place the label 'schizophrenia' into the diagnostic dustbin, in which it most certainly belongs, is not based solely on the poor science that surrounds it but also on the immense damage that this label can bring about. A single word can ruin a life as surely as any bullet and schizophrenia is just such a word.
>
> (Hammersley and McLaughlin, 2007)

CASL is by no means supported by the mental health system in general or many of the other mental health campaigning bodies. In particular those who subscribe to the brain disease model are concerned that it would be very difficult 'to raise awareness and fund research into the causes of an illness which doesn't exist or which has become too bland a word' (Marjorie Wallace, chief executive of SANE, quoted in *The Guardian*, 2007).

What CASL and the plethora of other service-user organizations represent is active resistance to the stigma of mental illness and to the discrimination and exclusion of service users. This challenge has had a profound impact upon the lives of service users and the cultural representation of mental illness.

The voice of the service user now demands respect and users are active stakeholders in the framework of the mental health care system. This ensures that services are more aware of and responsive to their needs and less stigmatizing as a result. There are also increasing opportunities for current and ex-service users to participate in mainstream society through supported housing, social support and employment schemes, and legislation that offers them some protection from discrimination. Many of these advances have resulted from the user-led organizational challenge.

Participation in organizations campaigning for change and support results in service users becoming advocates for social change and this enhances their empowerment. It encourages discourse about mental health and in so doing takes mental illness out of the hidden and murky shadows into an environment in which openness and empathy are encouraged.

Participation challenges the shame associated with mental illness and enhances the self-esteem of service uers, some of whom have felt sufficiently confident to reappropriate stigmatized labels. Parallells have been drawn with the gay movement in that it is noted that an increasing number of mental health service users are 'coming out of the closet' (Hinshaw, 2007: ix).

Not all mental health service users are involved with user movements and as noted in Chapter 3 there are concerns about under-representation of some groups. There are also concerns that the former radicalism is being replaced by users becoming 'mainstreamed' as they are incorporated into mental health care policy and co-opted into decision-making structures and service delivery.

Although the organizational challenge appears to have had some success in tackling stigma and discrimination effectively, there is still a long way to go. Prejudicial attitudes towards some mental health service users are still prevalent and a desire for social distance from certain disorders still persists. The challenge has yet to result in a stigma-free and socially inclusive environment for service users but it has irrefutably had an impact.

7 Is the end of stigma associated with long-term conditions in sight?

The previous chapters have examined the concept of stigma and how it is changing and being challenged in three contemporary contexts involving long-term conditions. This final chapter asks what these challenges amount to and returns to the question posed at the opening of the book – are we arriving at 'the end of stigma?'

The chapter begins by revisiting the discussion about the theoretical validity of the stigma concept and then goes on to assess how effective the three challenges have been. A discussion about the relationship between discrimination and disadvantage follows, drawing upon findings from a study focusing on the experiences of people with MS.[1] The final section revisits the question posed in the title of the book:

Key features of stigma revisited

Stigma and the capacity to divide people into 'insiders' and 'outsiders', those who belong and those who do not, has long been a feature of human societies. But at the heart of stigma lies the idea that society contains a set of big-scale, relatively abstract prejudicial concepts that are shared by large numbers of individuals and serve to define majority groups in opposition to minorities.

The hallmark of late modern societies, however, is their tendency towards an increasing diversification of roles and identities coupled with an intensification of reflexivity, self-awareness, choice and narrative control over individual biography. In such a kaleidoscopic socio-cultural context, defining who belongs to which group becomes both increasingly difficult and decreasingly relevant, as group membership itself is in a state of constant flux. If all of us (or none) are 'available' to be stigmatized, the concept itself begins to dissolve.

Goffman was well aware of the contextual and relative nature of stigma whereby identities and behaviours that are stigmatized in one context may be deemed neutral or even revered elsewhere. He was writing, though, about a society in which relationships seemed sufficiently fixed in any given context to make the distinction between 'us' and 'them' relatively stable and thus make stigma a meaningful concept. In the current context, however, post-modern analyses indicate that the big battalions that made up modern society are fracturing and identities are no longer fixed but increasingly flexible, shifting and unpredictable. As we have seen, this complexity is evident in the cultural sphere, where social behaviours such as legal and illegal intoxication may be simultaneously vilified and punished on the one hand and applauded and rewarded on the other, or in which people with long-term conditions may be shunned or lionized. In such an increasingly complex cultural milieu, stigma may become too slippery a concept and cease to be a useful tool for the interpretation of social relationships. Under these conditions, would it not make more sense to focus our attention on power, discrimination and exclusion as the essential social facts defining public relationships?

Colin Sumner in his provocatively titled book *The Sociology of Deviance: An Obituary* charts the life of 'deviance' as a field of academic study from its birth with the publication of Durkheim's *Rules of the Sociological Method* in 1895 to its 'death' with the publication of a number of texts in 1975 'which effectively killed off the field' (Sumner, 1994: vii). Sumner uses the metaphor of warfare to describe the demise of deviance whereby the combatants in their enthusiastic debates to define, delimit and develop the ideological basis of deviance effectively demolish it:

> The terrain now resembles the Somme in 1918. It is barren, fruitless, full of empty trenches and craters, littered with unexploded mines and eerily silent. No one fights for hegemony over a dangerous graveyard. It is now time to drop arms and show respect for the dead.
>
> (ibid.: ix)

In his epitaph Sumner lists the shortcomings of the concept of social deviance, including a lack of a normative consensus against which deviance is set; incoherent relations between deviance, crime and difference whereby 'What [is] defined as criminal, deviant or different [is] all beginning to look very arbitrary' (ibid.: 310); and a fruitless endeavour to identify a general theory of deviance.

Sumner's obituary to deviance as a field of sociological study has parallels with Fukuyama's 'end of history' in the political and economic arena and much of Sumner's critique could indeed be applied to the concept of stigma. The lack of normative consensus about what and who is stigmatized in which contexts means that it becomes ever more difficult to define. The stigma concept has also been criticized for both its individualism and its lack of definitional clarity. Furthermore, as the literature on stigma increasingly focuses upon more macro concerns relating to discrimination and social exclusion, the distinction between 'stigma', 'discrimination', 'prejudice' and 'social exclusion' becomes blurred and the terms are frequently used interchangeably (see Sayce, 1998). Recent articles have aimed to advance the field through cross-disciplinary endeavours to 'tease apart' and explain the linkages between stigma, prejudice and discrimination (Pescosolido, Martin, Lang and Olafsdottir, 2008; Phelan *et al.*, 2008; Stuber *et al.*, 2008), but this endeavour for definitional clarity suggests that the stigma concept, although not yet dead, is no longer in its prime.

Two recent influential articles about stigma identify power differentials as key to the process of stigma production (Link and Phelan, 2001; Parker and Aggleton, 2003) and this has now become an accepted element of the sociology of stigma. Because of this there have been calls for the social sciences to focus less upon individual stigma management and to shift the academic gaze towards examining the structural forces that underlie the power imbalances that lead to discrimination and social exclusion.

If power is the key to inclusion/exclusion then how do those with long-term conditions fare? Illness and disability not only affect the 'have-nots' and even the most resource-rich and powerful in society may be diagnosed with long-term conditions. Does a diagnosis of long-term illness inevitably lead to stigma, disempowerment, discrimination and downward social drift? Not necessarily, it would seem, and whereas those with most resources and power invariably have more protection against social exclusion, an ever greater proportion of people with long-term conditions are able to retain their social position.

An important adjunct to this is the changing age profile of the population in high-income countries. Average life expectancy continues to rise and as a result there are growing numbers of old and very old people, who are more likely to have or develop long-term conditions than younger people. In the 2001 UK census 18 per cent of the population reported a long-term illness or disability that limited their daily activities in some respect and the proportion increased with age, further accelerating in later life (Office of National Statistics, 2008). The proportion of people with a limiting long-standing condition is expected to rise over the next 25 years (Department of Health, 2008b).

In addition, advanced diagnostic techniques and genetic tests that can identify vulnerability to certain conditions augment the growing proportion of people living with the spectre of long-term illness. People with long-term conditions represent an increasingly sizeable proportion of the population and, with the development of management techniques that help to slow down progression, mask symptoms and limit disability through the use of sophisticated technologies, we are indeed living in the 'remission society' identified by Frank (1995). This makes both the distinction between the 'ill' and the 'well' less clear-cut and less meaningful. In such a scenario, stigma associated with illness loses its potency.

How effective are the challenges to stigma?

Technological development

Since the dawn of the industrial era, technology has been widely seen as a panacea for a range of illnesses. The idea of a laboratory-developed 'cure' remains something of a 'holy grail' for both scientists and people with long-term illnesses alike. Even those people who have a positive approach to living with a long-term condition would, in the main, opt for a cure if it were available. Although dramatic recovery can entail a difficult readjustment to 'normal' life, it is generally welcomed. A UK broadsheet recently featured the case of Vicky Duncan, who was born with a degenerative condition affecting her retina so that her eyesight deteriorated from the age of 8 until her twenties, when she could see no more than the difference between light and dark (Moorhead, 2008). She underwent pioneering surgery in her mid-twenties, which largely restored her sight. Her improved vision took some time to adjust to, as she had to cope with seeing her family for the first time in years and her husband for the first time ever, as well as herself as an adult. However, in general her improved sight offered her greater opportunities and had a direct impact on her work by giving her the confidence to commute into London and find a new job with the Royal National Institute for Blind People.

This book has explored the dramatic impact of new technology in the form of highly active antiretroviral therapy (HAART) upon HIV-positive people. Since the introduction of HAART in 1996, many HIV-positive people who were ill and dying have seen great improvements to their health to the extent that they are able to re-engage with the labour market and other previously forgone activities of daily living. Those diagnosed since 1996 are able to sustain a relatively 'normal' life as HIV is now, in the main, a manageable long-term condition.

These technological advances have had a dramatic impact on the stigma and social exclusion associated with HIV because a far greater proportion of HIV-positive people have been able to make long-term plans and participate in social and economic life. It is worth noting, however, this has come about not by changing public attitudes, but through improved health and as a result of the greater opportunities for HIV-positive people to conceal their stigmata.

Although technology has had only a relatively limited impact in terms of addressing the underlying causes of HIV-related stigma, it nevertheless enables many HIV-positive people to mask their illness much more effectively, thus making HIV less salient to their public identity. In terms of stigma, the impact of HAART is that, by controlling progression, it allows for concealment. HIV-positive people using HAART look just like other people and are thus able to merge seamlessly with the rest of society.

This process actually poses no threat at all to existing socio-cultural values and prejudicial attitudes. Furthermore, it locates the cause of stigma in the impairment of the individual rather than the prejudicial attitudes of groups and societies. Technological challenges may thus be less enthusiastically received by activists campaigning against social oppression, as they recognize that these developments do little to challenge prejudicial and discriminatory ideologies.

Masking illness with technology also sits uneasily with the personal challenge, which embraces the illness identity. However, the complexity of this interface is well illustrated by the story of a young boy, Nathan, with Down's syndrome featured on a national television series, *Born to be Different*, about the lives of families with a disabled child (Channel 4, September 2007). As a result of his condition, Nathan had a protruding tongue that was highly visible, hindered his speech and was frequently commented on in a negative way by his peers. His parents decided to opt for an operation to remove a part of his tongue so that it would fit more easily into his mouth, which would facilitate clearer speech and make him look 'less different'. The mother, however, was clear that she did not wish to 'mask' the fact that he had Down's syndrome and was disparaging of parents who had put their child through what she felt was needless cosmetic surgery to make their child look 'normal'. As she said, 'Your child has an extra number 21 chromosome and no amount of surgery is going to remove that.' This bald statement clearly illustrates the limits of any technological fix, but it is still clear that medication or treatment that helps to mask a condition gives people more control over when, how and in what circumstances they disclose their health status. It is thus a potent and effective instrument in the management of a stigmatized condition.

Moral personal identity

The narrative construction of valued selfhood, underpinning the personal challenge to stigma, continually finds new outlets, especially as public fascination with 'illness stories' grows. One example is 'Baldy's Blog', the on-line diary of the late Adrian Sudbury, a young man diagnosed with two forms of leukaemia (Sudbury, 2008). He filmed his own bone marrow transplant and posted this and his diary that he kept during his treatment on his on-line blog so readers could 'journey through the ups and downs of leukaemia, its treatments, living and dying'. His blog was awarded a prize from the Guild of Health Writers for communicating about health issues and, in response to a further award from the European School of Oncology, a reader wrote, 'Yet more accolades Adrian!!! Not only are you a star in our country, you are applauded in Europe for what you have achieved, and no doubt there will be more awards to come.' His openness and honesty in terms of facing illness and death and his willingness to share the experience with a wider public have clearly counteracted any sense of inferiority and negative worth traditionally associated with long-term illness. This stands in contrast to those writing about the experience of long-term illness and disability in the 1960s cited in the introductory chapter of this book, who found the responses of others to them both stigmatizing and damaging to self-esteem. Adrian Sudbury had no fear of any potentially stigmatizing public response to his illness, but actively courted public support and gained strength from doing so. His blog sustained his sense of selfhood and worth and he warned his readers, 'As I keep saying – don't feel sorry for me. I'm having a blast.'

From time to time someone living with a long-term condition acquires a kind of 'hero' status through their appearance in the mass media. A recent striking example of the phenomenon is the case of Professor Randy Pausch, an American academic who died of pancreatic cancer on 25 July 2008. Initially, Professor Pausch achieved celebrity status through the millions of 'hits' on his lecture titled 'The Last Lecture: Really Achieving Your Childhood Dreams' on the internet site YouTube (Pausch, 2007). What is noteworthy about the case is that neither his lecture nor his subsequent best-selling book (Pausch and Zaslow, 2008) was about either his illness or his academic specialty. Rather, his position as a dying man appeared to confer on him a kind of moral authority that allowed him to lecture and write on how life should be lived by all of us.

Pride among people with certain conditions has long been identified. In the early 1980s a study of 200 deaf people noted that, when interacting with the hearing world, deaf people clearly articulated feelings of inferiority, but in other contexts they related strongly to a positive deaf identity:

> Deaf people from deaf families see themselves as carrying on a cultural tradition to which little or no stigma is attached. Instead, they have a strong and positive identification that carries them through life . . . American Sign Language is a symbolic badge of identity in the deaf community.
>
> (Becker, 1981: 22)

Further evidence of this is the heated debate that took place in the UK in December 2007 about whether deaf parents should be allowed to screen their embryos to select a deaf child. Jackie Ballard, the chief executive of the Royal National Institute for Deaf and Hard of Hearing People, said, 'Most parents would choose to have a hearing embryo, but for those few parents who do not, we think they should be allowed to exercise that choice and we would support them in that decision' (reported in the *Sunday Times*, 2007). The British Deaf Association is currently campaigning for a change in legislation in order to make it legal to select embryos with disabilities and argues that it is discriminatory not to have this choice.

The personal challenge has thus had a major impact upon the experience of living with a long-term condition. It provides a platform from which people can and do narrate biographies in which they construct an identity that is good, moral and proud. This is in clear opposition to, and challenges, the traditional stigmatized status of those with long-term conditions in which the self has been lost. The person, not the illness, now takes centre stage.

Anti-stigma action

The previous chapter analysed the depth and breadth of the organizational challenge to stigma in the field of mental health. Whilst mental health activists have played a pioneering role in the organizational challenge, similar action has been evident in relation to a myriad of other conditions and there are a host of campaigning organizations and disabled people's alliances. These aim to improve the quality of life of people with long-term conditions. This is achieved primarily through widening participation and social inclusion, either indirectly via improved treatment resulting in better health, which enables greater social participation, or directly through improved access to the built environment.

The work environment has been a key focus for attention in an attempt to increase the proportion of people with long-term conditions entering and/ or remaining in employment. The relationship between work and illness is discussed in newspaper articles such as a recent one titled 'Should you tell bosses and colleagues if you are diagnosed with a serious illness?' (*The Guardian*, 2008c) and there are a number of supportive guides for employers and employees such as *Working through Cancer: A Guide for Employees*, produced by Macmillan Cancer Support (2007). This includes the personal story of a woman returning to work following treatment for breast cancer, as well as advice on when to return to work and strategies to support this. A brief discussion of 'your rights at work' outlines relevant legislation whereby 'it is unlawful for an employer to treat you less favourably because of your cancer'.

This kind of increased awareness of and openness about illness and disability are also evident in, and promulgated by, the arts, with numerous events inspired by social aspects of the lived experience. A recent example is an exhibition held in Colchester, UK, entitled 'Life beyond the Label', with a subtitle 'before you make up your mind . . . open it', which aims to challenge stereotypes, explore prejudices and provoke debate about society's relationship with disability. The exhibition was created with input from disabled people and aimed to convey their essential personhood and everyday reality of living with disability. In an interactive exhibit entitled 'Who am I?', people describe themselves and reflect upon the 'fit' (or lack of it) between their 'label' and who they really are. The exhibition includes disability aids such as a stylish basketball wheelchair, with quotes such as 'I have a custom-made wheelchair, you can choose the colours and it can be part of your identity' to illustrate the relationship between disability aids and identity. This and other exhibits, such as a Paralympic Barbie doll, portray disabled people's identities as being much more than their label. It also directly challenges the visitor to question the stereotypes they hold about disabled people. Likewise a play entitled *Flower Girls* (Cameron, 2007) performed by GRAEae, a disabled-led theatre company, asks audiences to write messages 'saying how you would like attitudes toward disabled people to change in the future'.

Organizational challenges are diverse and operate on a number of levels, sometimes provoking heated debates between protagonists about what it is that is being aimed for. There was, for example, controversy about two HIV campaigns from California, one titled 'HIV (not fabulous)' and the other 'HIV is no picnic', which drew attention to lipodystrophy, diarrhoea and night sweats experienced by some HIV-positive people. The campaign was criticized for scaremongering and potentially discouraging people coming forward for testing and treatment. Yet campaigns based on HIV-positive people being athletic and super-active have also attracted criticism for downplaying the seriousness of the illness.

The long-term sustainability of political action based on 'identity' has been questioned, as identities are contestable and subject to change; as a result, in the political field, splinter groups develop that prioritize different identities (Lee, 2002). Furthermore many people with long-term illnesses do not want to identify themselves as 'disabled' and this creates a problem about how to build solidarity while at the same time championing diversity. There are also concerns about the representativeness of political action about illness and disability, as only a minority take part and ethnic minority groups, less educated and older people are under-represented, and potentially further marginalized as a result. However, in spite of such shortcomings and limitations it is clear that a huge amount has been achieved as a result of user-led activism. Society has yet to fully implement a social model of disability but it is hard to disagree with the words of influential disability theorists that 'the course of politics is flowing inexorably and irreversibly toward a changed consciousness by disabled people and of disabled people' (Shakespeare and Watson, 2001: 562).

Disentangling discrimination from disadvantage: the case of restricted opportunities of people with MS

If the premise that stigma and discrimination against people with long-term conditions are on the wane as a result of the challenges analysed in this book, then full citizenship should be an attainable goal. However, a number of obstacles have been identified. First, as Sayce (2000) has argued, we are still a long way from achieving citizenship in everyday life, at least for many mental health service users. Although stigma and discrimination associated with long-term conditions are undoubtedly being challenged it remains uncertain whether full citizenship will ever be achieved or whether the stigma of illness will ever be eliminated altogether. Following from this the second obstacle arises, namely that, even if stigma and discrimination are eliminated, there are some activities of daily life to which people with long-term conditions will always have restricted access. Not all people with long-term conditions, for example, can be integrated into employment. There are examples of people with severe impairments building prestigious careers, such as the scientist Stephen Hawking, who has become a world-renowned physicist despite requiring assistance with many activities of daily living as a result of progressive motor neurone disease. In the UK, government policy over the last decade has resulted in increasing numbers of people with long-term conditions being integrated into the world of work, but there remains a residual, reasonably sizeable group who have not been. There may also be restrictions to participation in other life domains such as housing or social activities.

In an attempt to explore such restrictions, I initiated a research project to assess the social and economic disruption resulting from multiple sclerosis (MS), and examined how this varied according to level of disability.[2] MS affects the central nervous system and is the most common disabling neurological disease among young adults. It is usually diagnosed between the ages of 20 and 40 and progresses at a highly variable rate leading to a range of diverse symptoms (see www.mssociety.org, accessed 9 July 2008). Typically, people are diagnosed with relapsing–remitting MS, in which relapses are followed by recovery and remission, although most will later develop secondary progressive MS, in which relapses result in permanent disability.[3] Some people with MS are only minimally affected, either on a temporary basis or in a minor way, whereas others progress rapidly and can become dependent on others for most activities of daily living. The majority of people with MS fall between these two extremes.

Our research examined the social and economic impact of MS upon households in a number of life domains. A systematic comparison between MS and non-MS households was conducted in order to compare social and economic indicators among households affected by MS and the general population (Green *et al.*, 2007). The items we examined were household composition; marital status; annual household income; and employment status.[4]

The results of the matched analysis showed that people with MS were significantly less likely to be employed and were more likely to have a 'below average' household income than those in the general population, despite the fact that they were better educated and were in a higher social class. Taking age, education and ethnic group into account, people with MS were about half as likely as the general population to be in paid employment and this impacted on the economic position of the household (Green *et al.*, 2007).

As well as this evidence of the negative impact of MS in terms of household income and employment, the study also found a set of relationships linking income and employment to the level of disability experienced by people with MS (Green *et al.*, 2007). Other dimensions of life that were directly related to disability level were employment (both of the people with MS and of those around them), social and leisure activities, standard of living and intimate relationships (Green and Todd, 2008).

As part of this study respondents who reported an impact in any domain were asked for further comments. Analysis of these textual data suggested that the impact could be conceptualized in two inter-related themes: 'restricting choices' and 'limiting independence' for both people with MS and their households (Green and Todd, 2008).

The respondents described the process whereby the symptoms related to MS forced them to forgo a number of former activities and the subsequent narrowing of their participation in mainstream everyday activities as the illness progressed. In addition to restricted life opportunities they also recounted increased dependency on other people, particularly other family members, sometimes 'rely[ing] on others for almost everything'. This was described by one respondent as robbing her of her life, and a number commented about the negative impact on their identity that this engendered (Green and Todd, 2008).

This study thus confirms the social and economic impact of MS upon people with MS and their households in a number of domains and also shows how the impact significantly increases as disability and dependency become more pronounced. What is noteworthy in relation to the argument presented here is the extent to which this downward drift is related to the illness *per se* or to the stigma and discrimination that arise in response to the illness.

There is some evidence that MS is a stigmatized illness and, despite variations in speed and nature of MS progression, the general population still tends to associate the condition with disability and rapid and irreversible physical deterioration. The image of MS is often associated with a wheelchair and the cellist Jaqueline du Pré, whose brilliant career was cut short by MS and whose health declined fairly rapidly until her death at age 42. Her story accentuates the tragedy associated with long-term illness involving a ruined career, a talented life cut down in its prime and rapid onset of disability and dependency leading to eventual death. Campaigning groups are keen to move away from such negative images and present life with MS in a far more positive, upbeat light. 'When I was told I had MS I thought it was terminal, but there's life after diagnosis' says a person with MS quoted in a recent advertisement from the MS Society, and its national advertising campaign titled 'Putting the Pieces Together' is about living with MS and focuses on sex and relationships, socializing and lifestyle, and the world of work.

MS is different in a number of respects from the conditions discussed in Chapters 3–5. First, for many people with MS it is not possible to hide the symptoms of the illness as speech may be slurred, mobility reduced and co-ordination poor, often requiring the use of visible disability aids. Such symptoms have the potential to disrupt or lead to awkward social interactions. Second, MS causality is unclear although it is thought to be related to genetic composition and environmental triggers, neither of which are associated with blame. It is not an illness that targets specific groups, nor is it associated with particular lifestyles, so people with MS are not generally perceived as blameworthy for their condition. Thus the stigma associated with MS is related to aesthetic considerations and difference rather than danger, deviance or blame.

In the textual data we gathered in our MS study some respondents alluded to the stigma of MS. They reported discrimination in the workplace, with one respondent saying, 'I was fired as a public liability risk the day after my diagnosis'. Others reported that they felt discriminated against on the basis of their medical history or reported that for fear of any discrimination they 'never disclosed fact that I had MS so had to lie about health'. Non-disclosure and shame led others to avoid social contact, with one respondent writing that they '[did] not have a social life, like to keep my disability problems inside – not good at showing my disability'. They also reported that other household members had been affected by courtesy stigma; one woman wrote that as a result of her symptoms her children were 'teased at school', and another that 'some people [are] embarrassed in being with me when using [my] scooter'. And there were also occasionally reports of being rejected by former contacts, with one respondent writing, 'A couple of my friends, one in particular who I've known for over 25 years, have turned away.'

Experiences of stigma and the need for stigma management strategies are confirmed in other studies. The process of managing stigma in social interactions can be so demanding that people with MS report that the process can make them 'feel more ill' and requires strategies to reaffirm their sense of self and identity (Grytten and Maseide, 2006). Thus a common tactic among people with MS is to conceal their condition to protect their sense of selfhood and their access to social participation and work (Grytten and Maseide, 2005).

Thus stigma is clearly an important consideration for some people with MS. However, in the responses we received, whereas there were numerous references to limitations as a result of the *physical consequences* of MS, there were only occasional references to the *social consequences* resulting from others' response to the illness. Restricted access and opportunities were mainly related to impairment rather than to stigma. One man, for example, whose vision was poor as a result of a number of episodes of optic neuritis (a common symptom of MS) had had to give up his work as a taxi driver on account of safety considerations rather than any stigma associated with his restricted vision. Although the area between what someone is able to do and what they are not is clouded by stereotypes about illness and disability, and people with long-term conditions may be unjustifiably restricted from certain activities, it nevertheless remains that there are some activities or occupations to which people with some conditions may be unsuited.

Although much can and has been done to make the environment more accessible to disabled people, and there is still much more that could be done to enable people with a range of impairments to integrate into employment and other activities, there are some limits to participation. It is clear that 'full integration of impaired people in social production can never constitute the future to which all disabled people can aspire' (Abberley, 2002: 135).

The end of stigma in sight?

To conclude, I return to the question that forms the title of this book: to what extent do the challenges described in this book represent at least the beginning of the end of stigma associated with long-term conditions?

Table 7.1 summarizes the challenges to stigma I have presented in the previous chapters.

The first row details the biomedical origin underlying the technological challenge. Disease is accompanied by symptoms, many of which make the person look 'different' and this is an important source of stigma. Technological advances mean that symptoms may be better controlled and become less noticeable to such an extent that a person with a disease may 'pass as normal'. This does nothing to address the ideological basis of stigma but it minimizes the visible impact and is clearly a highly effective method of avoiding stigma. There are of course limits and not all people will ever be able to avoid all visible stigmata but it can nevertheless act as an effective camouflage to give people greater control over the timing and manner of disclosure to others. Technology will perhaps therefore never lead to an end of stigma but it is a helpful hand-maiden to deflect stigmatizing responses from others.

The second row focuses upon illness and the perception and presentation of the self, which is the mechanism whereby people with long-term conditions can feel inferior to others, resulting in self-stigma, even leading to 'loss of self'. The personal challenge tackles this 'head-on' through narrative construction projecting a positive self that is demonstrably as good as others. In so doing, one rejects stereotypes and labels associated with long-term conditions as unjustified and not applicable to the self. Self-esteem is maintained, the internalization of stigma is resisted and self-identity remains intact. It is thus an effective method for resisting the negative sequelae of self-stigma

Table 7.1 Challenges to stigma

Level of stigma	Essential character of stigma	Challenge to stigma	Principal impact of the challenge
Perception of others	They see me as inferior	Technological	They can't tell the difference between me and others
Perception of self	I feel inferior	Personal	I feel as good as others because I *am* as good as others
Perception of society	They treat us as inferior	Organizational	We are citizens, we qualify for equal rights and we will fight for them

and, even though stigmatization may still occur, the personal challenge provides effective armour to minimize the wounds it may cause.

Yet the personal challenge is rooted in the individual and thus has limited impact on structural conditions and power differentials that lie at the heart of stigma and wider discrimination. These can be challenged most effectively by political action or the organizational challenge (the third row in Table 7.1). The social response to sickness leads to stigmatization based on the premise that those who are ill are inferior or, to quote Goffman (1963: 3), 'reduced in our minds from a whole and usual person to a tainted, discounted one'. There is growing resistance at a political and societal level to the designation that people with long-term conditions are unworthy, and there is increased political action by those with long-term conditions to address the macro social and economic structures that enable the process of stigmatization to unfold. Sick and disabled people are asserting their rights as citizens; this provides an effective weapon against, and has had a major impact upon, the stigma and social exclusion associated with illness.

The three challenges do not of course operate in isolation. Each is informed by and drives the others. Operating as a whole, they provide effective resistance to stigma and minimize the power and impact of stigma upon people living with a range of long-term conditions. Does this mean that in the future stigma associated with illness and disability will be consigned to the history books and that having a long-term condition will excite no more reaction or comment than someone wearing glasses in the current day? Although we are still some way from reaching such a nirvana, the first steps of the journey have plainly been taken. Stigma in relation to illness is still alive and kicking but it is facing major assaults on all fronts. Its days may well be numbered.

Notes

1 Challenging stigma

1 The World Health Organization defines long-term conditions as health problems that require ongoing management over many years or decades. This includes a wide range of health conditions such as cancer, cardiovascular disease, HIV/AIDS, long-term mental disorders such as schizophrenia and depression as well as ongoing impairments such as blindness or joint disorders.

2 Stigma

1 A cross-disciplinary 'Health & Society Scholars Working Group on Stigma, Prejudice and Discrimination' met in September 2006 to try to integrate social and psychological understanding of stigma and prejudice. The papers presented were collated into a Special Issue of the journal *Social Science & Medicine* (volume 67, issue 3, published in August 2008).
2 Felt stigma is sometimes referred to as 'perceived stigma'.
3 Link and Phelan use the term 'label' rather than 'attribute' or 'condition' as a 'label' is something that is affixed by others and may or may not have validity.
4 However, the 'absence of the body' in disability theory has been criticized and there are calls, particularly from disabled women writers, to 'bring impairment back in'. According to Morris, 'While environmental barriers and social attitudes are a crucial part of our experience of disability – and do indeed disable us – to suggest that that is all there is to it is to deny the personal experience of physical and intellectual restrictions, of illness, of the fear of dying' (Morris, 1991: 10).
5 Research into stigma, however, remains vibrant among some groups such as the Chicago Consortium for Stigma Research, which includes 25 researchers in seven universities and conducts over 60 projects associated with the stigma of mental illness (Corrigan, 2005). Also, as noted above, there is renewed enthusiasm for cross-disciplinary work which attempts to advance conceptual models of stigma and prejudice through integrating social and psychological approaches (see Stuber, Meyer and Link, 2008).

3 Technological, personal and organizational challenges to stigma and exclusion

1 A perusal of a weekly TV guide in February 2008 showed for example that Channel 4 screened a reality programme *Supersize vs Superskinny* in which clinically underweight and overweight people swap lifestyles. This was followed the same evening by a *Bodyshock* special called 'The Girl with 8 Limbs' (on 19 February 2008). The following night Channel 5 screened *Extraordinary People: The Boys Joined at the Head*. Such programmes have become so popular that they are parodied in comedy shows such as *That Mitchell and Webb Look*, which on 22 February 2008 included a spoof documentary called 'A Boy with an Arse for a Face'.
2 In contrast to this, there are also examples of people actively resisting a close association between their illness and their identity. Kelly, for example, shows how people with ileostomies experience them as being attached to an alien object that is not part of the self (Kelly, 1992).
3 Although service-user involvement has been criticized as being tokenistic, it nevertheless becomes an ever more central part of health and social care policy and practice in the UK.

4 There are many other examples, such as 'Race for Life', a women-only fund-raising event that has as an annual target to raise £50 million to support the prevention and treatment of cancer (see www.raceforlife.org/raisingmoney/).

5 Peer support and techniques to address uncertainty and anxiety as well as developing effective communication with family, friends and health professionals are key elements.

6 The Disability Discrimination Act when it first appeared was criticized by the disability movement on a number of grounds. It was felt to be based on an individual medical approach. To qualify as disabled the impairment had to be proven and there were significant exclusions, e.g. mental health service users without a 'clinically well-recognized' impairment. Its jurisdiction did not cover employers of fewer than 20 people and it began life with no enforcement agency (Barnes and Mercer, 2003). Subsequent amendments have included an extension of its definition of disability to include people with HIV, cancer and multiple sclerosis from the point of diagnosis, rather than from the point when the condition has some adverse effect on ability to carry out normal day-to-day activities. There is also now an enforcement agency.

4 The technological challenge to stigma

1 This treatment was first referred to as 'combination therapy' and more recent names and acronyms have included 'antiretroviral therapy' (ART), 'highly active antiretroviral therapy' (HAART), and 'combination antiretroviral therapy' (CART).

2 The first study was funded by the Medical Research Council of Great Britain and carried out when I worked at the MRC Medical Sociology Unit, Glasgow University, 1990–95. I also draw upon a scoping exercise I conducted that was funded by the British HIV Association in 2003.

3 Initially, the disease was so strongly linked with gay men that it was referred to as 'GRID' (gay-related immune deficiency), or 'gay cancer'.

4 All names used are pseudonyms.

5 The information about HIV treatment was mainly derived from the following websites: www.bhiva.org, accessed 14 June 2008; www.avert.org, accessed 20 June 2008; www.who.int/hiv/topics, accessed 20 June 2008.

6 HIV works by replicating itself and as it does so it can mutate and develop new strains that may be resistant to the treatment. HAART may fail if resistance develops although this may be resolved through a different combination of anti-HIV drugs. The effectiveness of HAART may also be compromised through interactions with other pharmaceuticals or recreational drugs.

7 The term 'black Africans' is used in this chapter as it is the terminology used for ethnic monitoring of HIV by disease surveillance centres in the UK. Since 2001, 'black Africans' are the ethnic group in which most new HIV infections have been diagnosed in the UK (see Green and Smith, 2004).

8 There is an interesting literature about the impact upon emotional intimacy (Beckerman, 2002) and the extent to which couples affected by HIV share the view that AIDS is a controllable chronic illness (Hoy-Ellis and Fredriksen-Golden, 2007).

9 Although HIV-positive people living in Europe, North America and Australia in theory have access to a health care system that treats HIV with HAART, access can be a problem for those living in marginalized circumstances (asylum seekers, drug users, homeless people or prisoners) who have limited capacity for controlling their lives and whose opportunities to access services are subsequently reduced (Takahashi, Wiebe and Rodriguez, 2001).

5 The personal challenge to stigma

1 Green, G., Smith, R. and South, N., 'A follow up study of individuals assessed by a Criminal Justice Mental Health Team', funded by NHS Eastern Region 2000–2003. Criminal Justice Mental Health Teams were set up in response to the Reed report (Reed Committee, 1992), which advised that prison is often an unsuitable, health-damaging environment for mentally disordered offenders and that treatment from health and social services is more appropriate. In response to the report, schemes were set up throughout the country to divert mentally disordered offenders to health and social services at first point of contact with police, while in custody, at court or in prison.

2 According to Gossop (2007: 180) *The Traffic in Narcotics* may 'legitimately lay claim to the title of the worst book written about drugs'.

3 All names used are pseudonyms.

4 A more comprehensive analysis of these narratives, on which this section is based, may be found in Green, Smith and South (2006).

5 Whereas some experienced prison as a safe place, offering opportunities to relax, reflect and even rebuild self-esteem, not all respondents had positive experiences. Indeed, negative prison experiences were sometimes drawn upon in 'out of control' narratives. Three respondents, for example, claimed to have acquired a heroin addiction while in prison and another said he was able to withstand a prison sentence only by using heroin.

6 Klockars (1974) developed the concept 'metaphor of ledger' to describe individuals' justification for deviant behavior by claiming that their essential decency and goodness outweighs any negative acts or badness. As 'Vincent' tells Klockars (1974: 151) 'you gotta take into account all the things in my life and put 'em together, no doubt about it, I gotta come out on the good side'. Klockars noted that in general people judge themselves to be, on balance, 'good'.

6 The organizational challenge to stigma

1 The term 'service user' is the term generally used in this book to denote people with mental health problems as it is relatively neutral and most of the evidence that is discussed relates to people with mental health problems who are in contact with services.

2 The study was funded by a grant from the North East Essex Mental Health NHS Trust in 2000.

3 Although the evidence is strong that prejudicial attitudes towards mental health service users are pervasive, it is not clear whether or not this leads directly to discriminatory behaviour towards them. What people say about an 'out-group' and how they react when they have social contact with them may be quite different (see for example La Piere, 1934). However, there is some evidence that those with prejudicial attitudes are more likely to exhibit discriminatory behaviour (Corrigan, Edwards, Green, Thwart and Penn, 2001b).

4 A general population survey in Israel showed that, although many people showed a great deal of liberalism, tolerance and a socially inclusive attitude toward the mentally ill, they also demonstrated fear, distrust and rejection concerning actual involvement with them (Rahav, Struening and Andrews, 1984).

5 They included 15 who had recently been discharged from in-patient care and 12 who were attending a Mind drop-in centre. Sixteen were living independently, seven in supported accommodation and four were in a hostel for the homeless at time of interview. The interviews covered the quantity and quality of social ties and the perceived response to mental illness, especially processes of marginalization, stigma and discrimination. For further details see (Green, Hayes,

Dickinson, Whittaker and Gilheany, 2002; Green, Hayes, Dickinson, Whittaker and Gilheany, 2003).

6 All names used are pseudonyms.

7 According to Schulze and Angermeyer (2003: 303), 'there was agreement among the patients that one single contact with psychiatry was sufficient to put a life-long stamp on them, a stigma, which, in turn, determined their social identity in various interaction situations they entered'.

8 This was the slogan on a badge for sale at the 1995 conference of the National Association of Rights Protection and Advocacy. Other badges read, 'You bet I'm non-compliant and inappropriate' and 'Go manage your own case and get off mine' (all cited in Sayce, 2000: 116).

9 A critical analysis of the policy document upon which the 'Changing Minds' campaign was based suggests that the campaign also served the interests of the psychiatric profession (Pilgrim and Rogers, 2005). By linking stigma to specific psychiatric diagnoses, the campaign was based on a clinical model and the social phenomena at the heart of stigma were downplayed.

10 According to Navon the medical image of the campaign derived from science was at odds with the metaphorical use of leprosy in the spoken language, and scientific classification 'cannot uproot metaphorical classifications', making campaigns 'powerless in the face of language-based stigmatisation' (Navon, 1996: 269).

11 The local Government and Public Involvement in Health Act 2007 states clearly the obligation of National Health Service bodies to involve and consult patients and the public in the planning and provision of services.

12 There are similar campaigning groups in other parts of the world and in Japan the word 'schizophrenia' has been replaced with the term 'integration disorder'.

7 Is the end of stigma associated with long-term conditions in sight?

1 The study titled 'The disruption of multiple sclerosis upon the household' was funded by a grant from the Multiple Sclerosis Society 2003–4. This chapter draws upon the data from this study, much of which has already been published in two articles (Green and Todd, 2008; Green, Todd and Pevalin, 2007)

2 See note 1.

3 There are also two other types of MS: benign MS, which refers to a small number of relapses followed by a complete or almost complete recovery and no permanent disability, and primary progressive MS, in which symptoms and disability steadily increase.

4 The MS sample came from randomly selected members of the UK MS Society and those accessing the MS Society website, all of whom completed a self-completion questionnaire. Data for the general population came from the 2001/02 British General Household Survey (GHS). Cases from the MS Society sample were matched using propensity scoring with cases from the General Household Survey (see Green *et al.*, 2007).

References

Abberley, P. 2002, 'Work, disability, disabled people and European social theory', in *Disability Studies Today*, C. Barnes, M. Oliver and L. Barton, eds, Blackwell Publishers, Oxford, pp. 120–138.

Ablon, J. 1981, 'Dwarfism and social identity: self-help group participation', *Social Science & Medicine*, vol. 15B, pp. 25–30.

Ablon, J. 1995, ' "The elephant man" as "self" and "other": the psychosocial costs of a misdiagnosis,' *Social Science & Medicine*, vol. 40, pp. 1481–1489.

Adam, B. D., Maticka-Tyndale, E. and Cohen, J. J. 2003, 'Adherence practices among people living with HIV', *AIDS Care*, vol. 15, no. 2, pp. 263–274.

Ahern, J., Stuber, J. and Galea, S. 2007, 'Stigma, discrimination and the health of illicit drug users', *Drug and Alcohol Dependence*, vol. 88, no. 2–3, pp. 188–196.

AIDSmeds (2006) Can lipodystrophy be treated? Online. Available at: www.aidsmeds.com/articles/Lipodystrophy_10732.shtml (accessed 22 July 2008).

Albrecht, G. L., Walker, V. G. and Levy, J. A. 1982, 'Social distance from the stigmatized: a test of two theories', *Social Science & Medicine*, vol. 16, no. 14, pp. 1319–1327.

Albrecht, G. L., Seelman, K. and Bury, M. 2001, 'Introduction: the formation of disability studies', in *Handbook of Disability Studies*, G. L. Albrecht, K. Seelman and M. Bury, eds, Sage, London and New York, pp. 1–8.

Alonzo, A. and Reynolds, N. 1995, 'Stigma, HIV and AIDS: an exploration and elaboration of a stigma trajectory', *Social Science & Medicine*, vol. 41, pp. 303–315.

Altman, B. 2001, 'Disability definitions, models, classification schemes, and applications', in *Handbook of Disability Studies*, G. L. Albrecht, K. Seelman and M. Bury, eds, Sage, London and New York, pp. 97–121.

American Psychiatric Association 2000, *Diagnostic and Statistical Manual of Mental Disorders*, fourth edition – text revision (DSM-IV-TR), American Psychiatric Association, Arlington, VA.

American Society for Plastic Surgeons 2004, Innovative plastic surgery procedure rejuvenates HIV patients (press release 5 January 2004). Online. Available at: www.plasticsurgery.org/media/press_releases/Innovative-Plastic-Surgery-Procedure-Rejuvenates-HIV-Patients.cfm (accessed 4 August 2008).

Anderson, J. and Doyal, L. 2004, 'Women from Africa living with HIV in London: a descriptive case study', *AIDS Care*, vol. 16, no. 1, pp. 95–105.

Anderson, R. and Bury, M. (eds) 1988, *Living with Chronic Illness: The Experience of Patients and their Families*, Unwin Hyman, London.

Anderson, W. and Weatherburn, P. 1998, *The Impact of Combination Therapy on the Lives of People with HIV*, Sigma Research, London.

Anderson, W. and Weatherburn, P. 1999, *Taking Heart? The Impact of Combination Therapy on the Lives of People with HIV*, Sigma Research, London.

Angell, B., Cooke, A. and Kovak, K. 2005, 'First person accounts of stigma,' in *On the Stigma of Mental Illness: Practical Strategies for Research and Social Change*, P. Corrigan, ed., American Psychological Association, Washington DC, pp. 69–98.

Angermeyer, M. and Matschinger, H. 1996, 'The effect of violent attacks by schizophrenic persons on the attitude of the public towards the mentally ill', *Social Science & Medicine*, vol. 43, pp. 1721–1728.

Anspach, R. 1979, 'From stigma to identity politics: political activism among the physically disabled and former mental patients', *Social Science & Medicine*, vol. 13A, pp. 765–773.

Antiretroviral Therapy Cohort 2008, 'Life expectancy of individuals on combination antiretroviral therapy in high-income countries: a collaborative analysis of 14 cohort studies', *The Lancet*, vol. 372, pp. 293–299.

Apinundecha, C., Laohasiriwong, W., Cameron, M. and Lim, S. 2007, 'A community participation intervention to reduce HIV/AIDS stigma, Nakhon Ratchasima province, northeast Thailand', *AIDS Care*, vol. 19, no. 9, pp. 1157–1165.

Atrill, R., Kinniburgh, J. and Power, L. 2001, *Social Exclusion and HIV*, Terrence Higgins Trust, London.

Aylott, J. 1999, 'Should children with Down's syndrome have cosmetic surgery?', *British Journal of Nursing*, vol. 8, pp. 33–38.

Barnard, M. 2007, *Drug Addiction and Families*, Jessica Kingsley, London and Philadelphia.

Barnes, C. and Mercer, G. 2003, *Disability*, Polity Press, Cambridge.

Barnes, C., Oliver, M. and Barton, L. 2002, *Disability Studies Today*, Polity Press, Cambridge.

Barrington, C., Moreno, L. and Kerrigan, D. 2007, 'Local understanding of an HIV vaccine and its relationship with HIV-related stigma in the Dominican Republic', *AIDS Care*, vol. 19, no. 7, pp. 871–877.

Battye, L. 1966, 'The Chatterley syndrome', in *Stigma: The Experience of Disability*, P. Hunt, ed., Geoffrey Chapman, London, pp. 1–16.

BBC News 2006, Woman wins herceptin court fight. Online. Available at: http://news.bbc.co.uk/1/hi/health/4902150.stm (accessed 10 March 2008).

BBC Press Office 2004, Johnny Vegas plays Moz. Online. Available at: www.bbc.co.uk/pressoffice/pressreleases/stories/2004/12_december/13/ideal.shtml (accessed 18 June 2008).

Beck, U. 1992, *Risk Society*, Sage, London.

Becker, G. 1981, 'Coping with stigma: lifelong adaptation of deaf people', *Social Science & Medicine*, vol. 15B, pp. 21–24.

Beckerman, N. L. 2002, 'Couples coping with discordant HIV status', *AIDS Patient Care and STDs*, vol. 16, no. 2, pp. 55–59.

Bird, S. M. and Leigh-Brown, A. J. 2001, 'Criminalisation of HIV transmission: implications for public health in Scotland', *British Medical Journal*, vol. 323, no. 7322, pp. 1174–1177.

Blaxter, M. 2004, 'Life narratives, health and identity,' in *Identity and Health*, D. Kelleher and G. Leavey, eds., Routledge, London, pp. 170–199.

Brashers, D. E., Neidig, J. L., Cardillo, L. W., Dobbs, L. K., Russell, J. A. and Haas,

S. M. 1999, '"In an important way, I did die": uncertainty and revival in persons living with HIV or AIDS', *AIDS Care*, vol. 11, no. 2, pp. 201–219.

Brashers, D. E., Neidig, J. L., Russell, J. A., Cardillo, L. W., Haas, S. M., Dobbs, L. K., Garland, M., McCartney, B., and Nemeth, S. 2003, 'The medical, personal, and social causes of uncertainty in HIV illness', *Issues in Mental Health Nursing*, vol. 24, no. 5, pp. 497–522.

Brockington, I., Hall, P., Levings, J., and Murphy, C. 1993, 'The community's tolerance of the mentally ill', *British Journal of Psychiatry*, vol. 162, pp. 93–99.

Bromley, C., Ormston, R., and Scottish Executive Social Research Substance Misuse Research Programme 2005, *Part of the Scottish Way of Life? Attitudes Towards Drinking and Smoking in Scotland – Findings from the 2004 Scottish Social Attitudes Survey*, Edinburgh, Scottish Executive. Online. Available at: www.scotland. gov.uk/Publications/2005/07/2992847/28513 (accessed 28 April 2008).

Brown, H. 1966, 'Some anomalies of social welfare,' in *Stigma: The Experience of Disability*, P. Hunt, ed., Geoffrey Chapman, London, pp. 131–141.

Brown, P. and Zavestoski, S. 2004, 'Social movements in health: an introduction', *Sociology of Health and Illness*, vol. 26, no. 6, pp. 679–694.

Brown, P., Zavestoski, S., McCormick, S., Mayer, B., Morello, R. and Gasior Altman, R. 2004, 'Embodied health movements: new approaches to social movements in health', *Sociology of Health and Illness*, vol. 26, no. 1, pp. 50–80.

Bury, M. 1982, 'Chronic illness as biographical disruption', *Sociology of Health and Illness*, vol. 4, pp. 167–182.

Bury, M. 1991, 'The sociology of chronic illness: a review of research and prospects', *Sociology of Health and Illness*, vol. 13, pp. 451–468.

Bury, M. 1997, *Health and Illness in a Changing Society*, Routledge, London.

Byrne, P. 1997, 'Psychiatric stigma: past, passing and to come', *Journal of the Royal Society of Medicine*, vol. 90, pp. 618–621.

Byrne, P. 2001, 'Psychiatric stigma', *British Journal of Psychiatry*, vol. 178, pp. 281–284.

Cameron, R. 2007, *Flower Girls*, Methuen Drama, London.

Camp, D. L., Finlay, W. M. L. and Lyons, E. 2002, 'Is low self-esteem an inevitable consequence of stigma? An example from women with chronic mental health problems', *Social Science & Medicine*, vol. 55, no. 5, pp. 823–834.

Campbell, P. 1992, 'A survivor's view of community psychiatry', *Journal of Mental Health*, vol. 1, no. 2, pp. 117–122.

Carricaburu, D. and Pierret, J. 1995, 'From biographical disruption to biographical reinforcement: the case of HIV-positive men', *Sociology of Health and Illness*, vol. 17, pp. 65–88.

Castle, S. 2004, 'Rural children's attitudes to people with HIV/AIDS in Mali: the causes of stigma', *Culture, Health and Sexuality*, vol. 6, no. 1, pp. 1–18.

Catalan, J., Meadows, J. and Douzenis, A. 2000, 'The changing pattern of mental health problems in HIV infection: the view from London, UK', *AIDS Care*, vol. 12, no. 3, pp. 333–341.

Catalan, J., Green, L. and Thorley, F. 2003, 'The changing picture of HIV: a chronic illness, again?', *Focus: A Guide to AIDS Research and Counselling*, vol. 16, no. 3, pp. 1–4.

Centre for Economic Performance's Mental Health Policy Group 2006, *The Depression Report: A New Deal for Depression and Anxiety Disorders*, London School of Economics, London.

Charlton, J. 1998, *Nothing about Us Without Us: Disability, Oppression and Empowerment*, University of California Press, Berkeley.

Charmaz, K. 1983, 'Loss of self: a fundamental form of suffering in the chronically ill', *Sociology of Health and Illness*, vol. 5, pp. 168–195.

Child Welfare League of America 2001, *Alcohol, Other Drugs and Child Welfare*, Child Welfare League of America, Washington DC.

Chinouya, M. and Davidson, O. 2003, *The Padare Project: Assessing Health-Related Knowledge Attitudes and Behaviours of HIV-positive Africans Accessing Services in North Central London*, African HIV Policy Network, London.

City Press 2005, 'Australia denies HIV-positive Zambian a visa', *City Press Australia*, 11 November 2005.

Closer 2007, 'I'm proud of my booze blackouts', 24–30 November, pp. 24–25.

Cohen, J. and Struening, E. 1962, 'Opinions about mental illness in the personnel of two large hospitals', *Journal of Abnormal and Social Psychology*, vol. 64, pp. 349–360.

Cohen, S. 1985, *Visions of Social Control*, Polity Press, Cambridge.

Collins 2000, *Collins English Dictionary*, 5th edn, Harper Collins, Glasgow.

Conrad, P. 1987, 'The experience of illness: recent and new directions,' in *Research in the Sociology of Health Care, vol. 6: The Experience and Management of Chronic Illness*, J. Roth and P. Conrad, eds, JAI Press, Greenwich, CT, pp. 1–31.

Corrigan, P. (ed.) 2005, *On the Stigma of Mental Illness: Practical Strategies for Research and Social Change*, American Psychological Association, Washington DC.

Corrigan, P. and Cooper, A. 2005, 'Mental illness and dangerousness: fact or misperception, and implications for stigma,' in *On the Stigma of Mental Illness: Practical Strategies for Research and Social Change*, P. Corrigan, ed., American Psychological Association, Washington DC, pp. 165–179.

Corrigan, P. and Kleinlein, P. 2005, 'The impact of mental illness stigma,' in *On the Stigma of Mental Illness: Practical Strategies for Research and Social Change*, P. Corrigan, ed., American Psychological Association, Washington DC, pp. 11–44.

Corrigan, P. and Penn, D. 1999, 'Lessons from social psychology on discrediting psychiatric stigma', *American Psychologist*, vol. 54, pp. 765–776.

Corrigan, P. and Watson, A. 2002, 'The paradox of self-stigma and mental illness', *Clinical Psychology: Science and Practice*, vol. 9, pp. 35–53.

Corrigan, P. W., River, L. P., Lundin, R. K., Penn, D. L., Uphoff-Wasowski, K., Campion, J., Mathisen, J., Gagnon, C., Bergman, M., Goldstein, H. and Kubiak, M. A. 2001a, 'Three strategies for changing attributions about severe mental illness', *Schizophrenia Bulletin*, vol. 27, no. 2, pp. 187–195.

Corrigan, P., Edwards, A., Green, A., Thwart, S. and Penn, D. 2001b, 'Prejudice, social distance, and familiarity with mental illness', *Schizophrenia Bulletin*, vol. 27, no. 2, pp. 219–225.

Crandall, C. and Moriarty, D. 1995, 'Physical illness stigma and social rejection', *British Journal of Social Psychology*, vol. 34, pp. 67–83.

Crawford, R. 1994, 'The boundaries of self and the unhealthy other: reflections on health, culture and AIDS', *Social Science & Medicine*, vol. 38, no. 10, pp. 1347–1365.

Creegan, D. 1966, 'Adapt or succumb,' in *Stigma: The Experience of Disability*, P. Hunt, ed., Geoffrey Chapman, London, pp. 109–122.

Crisp, A. 2000, 'Changing Minds: every family in the land. An update on the the College's campaign', *Psychiatric Bulletin*, vol. 24, pp. 267–268.

Crisp, A., Gelder, M., Rix, S., Meltzer, H. and Rowlands, O. 2000, 'Stigmatisation of people with mental illness', *British Journal of Psychiatry*, vol. 177, pp. 4–7.

Crocker, J. and Major, B. 1989, 'Social stigma and self-esteem: the self-protective properties of stigma', *Psychological Review*, vol. 96, pp. 608–630.

Crocker, J., Major, B. and Steele, C. 1998, 'Social stigma,' in *The Handbook of Social Psychology* 2, D. T. Gilbert and S. T. Fiske, eds, McGraw-Hill, Boston, MA, pp. 504–553.

Crossley, M. L. 1997, ' "Survivors" and "victims": long-term HIV positive individuals and the ethos of self-empowerment', *Social Science & Medicine*, vol. 45, no. 12, pp. 1863–1873.

Crossley, M. L. 1998, ' "Sick role" or "empowerment"? The ambiguities of life with an HIV positive diagnosis', *Sociology of Health and Illness*, vol. 20, no. 4, pp. 507–531.

Crossley, M. L. 2003, ' "Let me explain": narrative emplotment and patient's experience of oral cancer', *Social Science & Medicine*, vol. 56, pp. 439–448.

Crossley, N. 1999, 'Fish, field, habitus and madness: the first wave mental health users movement in Great Britain', *British Journal of Sociology*, vol. 50, no. 4, pp. 647–670.

Crossley, N. 2006, *Contesting Psychiatry: Social Movements in Mental Health*, Routledge, London.

Daily Mail 2007 'False HIV diagnosis makes man run away and live on berries in a forest', 7 August.

Davis, K. K., Davis, J. S. and Dowler, L. 2004, 'In motion, out of place: the public space(s) of Tourette Syndrome', *Social Science & Medicine*, vol. 59, no. 1, pp. 103–112.

Davis, M., Imrie, J., Stephenson, J., Davidson, O., Hart, G. and Williams, I. 2000, 'Living with HIV treatments and adherence: interim qualitative findings from a study of gay men with HIV and AIDS in London', paper presented at The British Psychological Society Annual Conference, Winchester, 13 April.

Davis, M., Hart, G., Imrie, J., Davidson, O., Williams, I. and Stephenson, J. 2002, ' "HIV is HIV to me": the meanings of treatment, viral load and reinfection for gay men living with HIV', *Health, Risk and Society*, vol. 4, no. 1, pp. 31–43.

De Jong, W. 1980, 'The stigma of obesity: the consequences of naive assumptions concerning the causes of physical deviance', *Journal of Health and Social Behavior*, vol. 21, pp. 75–87.

Del Vecchio Good, M., Munakata, T., Kobayashi, Y., Mattingly, C. and Good, B. 1994, 'Oncology and narrative time', *Social Science & Medicine*, vol. 38, pp. 855–862.

Demant, J. and Jarvinen, M. 2006, 'Constructing maturity through alcohol experience – focus group interviews with teenagers', *Addiction Research and Theory*, vol. 14, no. 6, pp. 589–602.

Deng, R., Li, J., Sringernyuang, L. and Zhang, K. 2007, 'Drug abuse, HIV/AIDS and stigmatisation in a Dai community in Yunnan, China', *Social Science & Medicine*, vol. 64, no. 8, pp. 1560–1571.

Department of Health 2001, *The Expert Patient: A New Approach to Chronic Disease Management for the 21st Century*, The Stationery Office, London.

Department of Health 2005, *HIV Infected Health Care Workers: Guidance on Management and Patient Notification*, The Stationery Office, London.

Department of Health 2007a, *Raising the Profile of Long Term Conditions Care: A Compendium of Information*, The Stationery Office, London.

Department of Health 2007b, *Drug Misuse and Dependence: Guidelines on Clinical Management*, The Stationery Office, London. Online. Available at: www.nta.nhs.uk/areas/clinical_guidance/clinical_guidelines/docs/clinical_guidelines_2007.pdf (accessed 30 April 2008).

Department of Health 2008a, Patient and public empowerment. Online. Available at: www.dh.gov.uk/en/Managingyourorganisation/PatientAndPublicinvolvement/index.htm (accessed 23 May 2008).

Department of Health 2008b, Long term conditions. Online. Available at: www.dh.gov.uk/en/Healthcare/Longtermconditions/DH_084294 (accessed 24 April 2008).

Diamond, J. 1998, *C: Because Cowards Get Cancer Too . . .*, Vermilion, London.

Dray-Spira, R. and Lert, F. 2003, 'Social health inequalities during the course of chronic HIV disease in the era of highly active antiretroviral therapy', *AIDS*, vol. 17, no. 3, pp. 283–290.

Durkheim, E. 1964, *The Rules of the Sociological Method*, 8th edn, Free Press, New York.

Elias, N. and Scotson, J. L. 1994, *The Established and the Outsiders: A Sociological Enquiry into Community Problems*, 2nd edn, Sage, London.

Epstein, S. 1996, *Impure Science: AIDS, Activism and the Politics of Knowledge*, University of California Press, Berkeley.

Estroff, S. E. 1989, 'Self, identity and subjective experiences of schizophrenia: in search of the subject', *Schizophrenia Bulletin*, vol. 15, pp. 189–196.

Estroff, S. E., Penn, D. L. and Toporek, J. R. 2004, 'From stigma to discrimination: an analysis of community efforts to reduce the negative consequences of having a psychiatric disorder and label', *Schizophrenia Bulletin*, vol. 30, pp. 493–509.

Ezzy, D. 2000, 'Illness narratives: time, hope and HIV', *Social Science & Medicine*, vol. 50, no. 5, pp. 605–617.

Faircloth, C., Boylstein, C., Rittman, M., Young, M. and Gubrium, J. 2004, 'Sudden illness and biographical flow in narratives of stroke recovery', *Sociology of Health and Illness*, vol. 26, no. 2, pp. 242–261.

Falk, G. 2001, *Stigma: How We Treat Outsiders*, Prometheus Books, New York.

Featherstone, M. and Hepworth, M. 1991, 'The mask of ageing and the postmodern life course,' in *The Body: Social Processes and Cultural Theory*, M. Featherstone, M. Hepworth and B. Turner, eds, Sage, London.

Fennell, D. and Liberato, A. 2007, 'Learning to live with OCD: labeling, the self, and stigma', *Deviant Behavior*, vol. 28, pp. 305–331.

Fernandez, T. 2001, 'AIDS, combination therapy and survival', *Professional Nurse*, vol. 16, no. 10, pp. 1425–1428.

Ferrier, S. E. and Lavis, J. N. 2003, 'With health comes work? People living with HIV/AIDS consider returning to work', *AIDS Care*, vol. 15, no. 3, pp. 423–435.

Fife, B. L. and Wright, E. R. 2000, 'The dimensionality of stigma: a comparison of its impact on the self of persons with HIV/AIDS and cancer', *Journal of Health and Social Behavior*, vol. 41, no. 1, pp. 50–67.

Finkelstein, V. 1980, *Attitudes and Disabled People*, World Rehabilitation Fund, New York.

Fiske, S. 1998, 'Stereotyping, prejudice, and discrimination', in *The Handbook of Social Psychology*, D. T. Gilbert, S. T. Fiske and G. Lindzey, eds, McGraw-Hill, New York, pp. 357–411.

Flowers, P., Imrie, J., Hart, G. and Davis, M. 2003. Tensions in HIV management:

the role of innovative health technologies. Project no. L218 25 2011. Online. Available at: www.york.ac.uk/res/iht/projects/l218252011.htm (accessed 15 September 2008).

Flowers, P., Davis, M., Hart, G., Rosengarten, M., Frankis, J. and Imrie, J. 2006, 'Diagnosis and stigma and identity amongst HIV positive black Africans living in the UK', *Psychology and Health*, vol. 21, no. 1, pp. 109–122.

Ford, R. 1966, 'Quite intelligent,' in *Stigma: The Experience of Disability*, P. Hunt, ed., Geoffrey Chapman, London, pp. 29–43.

Foucault, M. 1978, 'About the concept of the "dangerous individual" in 19th century legal psychiatry', *International Journal of Law and Psychiatry*, vol. 1, pp. 1–18.

Foucault, M. 1988, 'The dangerous individual', in *Michel Foucault: Politics Philosophy Culture: Interviews and Other Writings 1977–1984*, L. Kritzman, ed., Routledge, London.

Frank, A. 1995, *The Wounded Storyteller: Body, Illness and Ethics*, University of Chicago Press, London.

Fukuyama, F. 1989, 'The end of history', *The National Interest,* Summer 1989, pp. 3–18.

Fukuyama, F. 1992, *The End of History and the Last Man*, Penguin, London.

Gallo, K. 1994, 'First-person account: self-stigmatization', *Schizophrenia Bulletin*, vol. 20, pp. 407–410.

Garmaise, D. 2002, 'Canada refuses to issue a visa to an HIV-positive worker on antiretroviral drugs', *Canadian HIV AIDS Policy Law Review*, vol. 7, pp. 24–25.

Giddens, A. 1991, *Modernity and Self-identity: Self and Society in the Late Modern Age*, Polity Press, Cambridge.

Gill, M. 1966, 'No small miracle', in *Stigma: The Experience of Disability*, P. Hunt, ed., Geoffrey Chapman, London, pp. 97–107.

Glanville, R. 1966, 'When the box doesn't fit,' in *Stigma: The Experience of Disability*, P. Hunt, ed., Geoffrey Chapman, London, pp. 68–80.

Goffman, E. 1959, *The Presentation of Self in Everyday Life*, Doubleday, Garden City, New York.

Goffman, E. 1961, *Asylums*, Doubleday, New York.

Goffman, E. 1963, *Stigma: Notes on the Management of Spoiled Identity*, Prentice-Hall, Englewood Cliffs, NJ.

Goffman, E. 1971, *Relations in Public: Microstudies of the Public Order*, Basic Books, New York.

Goldman, R. 2003, 'Being chronically ill', *Focus: A Guide to AIDS Research and Counselling*, vol. 16, no. 1, pp. 5–6.

Gossop, M. 2007, *Living with Drugs*, 6th edn, Ashgate Publishing, Aldershot, Hampshire.

Gove, W. 1982, 'Labeling theory's explanation of mental illness: an update of recent evidence', *Deviant Behavior*, vol. 3, pp. 307–327.

Gove, W. 2004, 'The career of the mentally ill: an integration of psychiatric labeling/ social construction, and lay perspectives', *Journal of Health and Social Behavior*, vol. 45, pp. 357–375.

Green, G. 1995, 'Attitudes towards people with HIV: are they as stigmatising as people with HIV think they are?', *Social Science & Medicine*, vol. 41, pp. 557–568.

Green, G. and Smith, R. 2004, 'The psychosocial and health care needs of HIV-positive people in the United Kingdom following HAART: a review', *HIV Medicine*, vol. 5, supplement 1, 1–46.

Green, G. and Sobo, E. J. 2000, *The Endangered Self: Managing the Social Risk of HIV*, Routledge, London.

Green, G. and Todd, J. 2008, '"Restricting choices and limiting independence": social and economic impact of MS upon households by level of disability', *Chronic Illness*, vol. 4, pp. 160–172.

Green, G., Hayes, C., Dickinson, D., Whittaker, A. and Gilheany, B. 2002, 'The role and impact of social relationships upon well-being reported by mental health service users: a qualitative study', *Journal of Mental Health*, vol. 11, pp. 565–579.

Green, G., Hayes, C., Dickinson, D., Whittaker, A. and Gilheany, B. 2003, 'A mental health service users perspective to stigmatisation', *Journal of Mental Health*, vol. 12, pp. 223–234.

Green, G., Smith, R. and South, N. 2005, 'Court-based psychiatric assessment: a case for an integrated diversionary and public health role', *Journal of Forensic Psychiatry and Psychology*, vol. 16, no. 3, pp. 577–591.

Green, G., Smith, R. and South, N. 2006, '"They say that you are a danger but you are not": representations and construction of the moral self in narratives of "dangerous individuals"', *Deviant Behavior*, vol. 27, no. 3, pp. 299–328.

Green, G., Todd, J. and Pevalin, D. 2007, 'Biographical disruption associated with multiple sclerosis: using propensity scoring to assess the impact', *Social Science & Medicine*, vol. 65, pp. 524–535.

Groce, N. 1985, *Everyone Here Spoke Sign Language: Hereditary Deafness on Martha's Vineyard*, Harvard University Press, Cambridge, MA.

Gronvik, L. 2007, 'The fuzzy buzz word: conceptualisations of disability in disability research classics', *Sociology of Health and Illness*, vol. 29, no. 5, pp. 750–766.

Grytten, N. and Maseide, P. 2005, '"What is expressed is not always what is felt": coping with stigma and the embodiment of perceived illegitimacy of multiple sclerosis', *Chronic Illness*, vol. 1, pp. 231–243.

Grytten, N. and Maseide, P. 2006, '"When I am together with them I feel more ill": the stigma of multiple sclerosis experienced in social relationships', *Chronic Illness*, vol. 2, pp. 195–208.

The Guardian 2007, 'Muddy thinking'. Online. Available at: www.guardian.co.uk/society/2007/oct/09/medicineandhealth (accessed 18 September 2008).

The Guardian 2008a, 'Doctors orders', 22 April.

The Guardian 2008b, 'Last night's TV: The Doctor Who Hears Voices'. Online. Available at: www.guardian.co.uk/culture/tvandradioblog/2008/apr/22/lastnightstvthedoctorwho (accessed 18 September 2008).

The Guardian 2008c, 'Should you tell bosses and colleagues if you are diagnosed with a serious illness?', 22 April.

Hall, P., Brockington, I., Levings, J. and Murphy, C. 1993, 'A comparison of responses to the mentally ill in two communities', *British Journal of Psychiatry*, vol. 162, pp. 99–108.

Hammersley, P. and McLaughlin, T. 2007, The campaign for abolition of the schizophrenia label. Online. Available at: www.asylumonline.net/ (accessed 6 August 2008).

Harley Medical Group 2008, Cosmetic surgery for women. Online. Available at: www.harleymedical.co.uk/cosmetic-surgery-for-women (accessed 20 June 2008).

Hassin, J. 1994, 'Living a responsible life: the impact of AIDS on the social identity of intravenous drug users', *Social Science & Medicine*, vol. 39, no. 3, pp. 391–400.

Hays, R., McKusick, L., Pollack, L., Hilliard, R., Hoff, C. and Coates, T. 1993, 'Disclosing HIV seropositivity to significant others', *AIDS*, vol. 7, pp. 425–431.

Health Education Authority 1997, *Young People's Resources to Combat Stigma Around Mental Health Issues: Qualitative Research to Evaluate Resource Materials*, Health Education Authority, London.

Herek, G. 1997, 'The HIV epidemic and public attitudes toward lesbians and gay men,' in *In Changing Times: Gay Men and Lesbians Encounter HIV/AIDS*, P. Levine, P. Nardi and J. H. Gagnon, eds, University of Chicago Press, Chicago, pp. 191–218.

Herek, G. and Capitanio, J. 1998, 'Symbolic prejudice of fear of infection? A functional analysis of AIDS-related stigma among heterosexual adults', *Basic and Applied Social Psychology*, vol. 20, pp. 230–241.

Herek, G. and Glunt, E. 1988, 'An epidemic of stigma: public reactions to AIDS', *American Psychologist*, vol. 43, no. 11, pp. 886–891.

Herek, G. M., Capitanio, J. P. and Widaman, K. F. 2002, 'HIV-related stigma and knowledge in the United States: prevalence and trends, 1991–1999', *American Journal of Public Health*, vol. 92, no. 3, pp. 371–377.

Herzlich, C. and Pierret, J. 1987, *Illness and Self in Society*, The Johns Hopkins University Press, Baltimore.

Hinshaw, S. 2007, *The Mark of Shame: Stigma of Mental Illness and an Agenda for Change*, Oxford University Press, Oxford.

Hogg, R. S., O'Shaughnessy, M. V., Gataric, N., Yip, B., Craib, K., Schechter, M. T. and Montaner, J. S. 1997, 'Decline in deaths from AIDS due to new antiretrovirals', *The Lancet*, vol. 349, no. 9061, p. 1294.

Home Office 2003, *Prevalence of Drug Use: Key Findings for the 2002/2003 British Crime Survey*, The Stationery Office, London. Online. Available at: www.homeoffice.gov.uk/rds/pdfs2/r229.pdf (accessed 22 May 2008).

Hosegood, V., Preston-Whyte, E., Busza, J., Moitse, S. and Timaeus, I. M. 2007, 'Revealing the full extent of households' experiences of HIV and AIDS in rural South Africa', *Social Science & Medicine*, vol. 65, no. 6, pp. 1249–1259.

Hosseinipour, M., Kazembe, P., Sanne, I. and van der Horst, C. 2002, 'Challenges in delivering antiretroviral treatment in resource poor countries', *AIDS*, vol. 16, Supplement 4, pp. S177–S187.

Hoy-Ellis, C. and Fredriksen-Golden, I. 2007, 'Is AIDS chronic or terminal? The perceptions of people living with AIDS and their informal support partners', *AIDS Care*, vol. 19, no. 7, pp. 835–843.

Hughes, E. 1945, 'Dilemmas and contradictions of status', *American Journal of Sociology*, vol. 50, pp. 353–359.

Hunt, P. (ed.) 1966a, *Stigma: The Experience of Disability*, Geoffrey Chapman, London.

Hunt, P. 1966b, 'A critical condition', in *Stigma: The Experience of Disability*, P. Hunt, ed., Geoffrey Chapman, London, pp. 143–159.

Huxley, P. and Thornicroft, G. 2003, 'Social inclusion, social quality and mental illness', *British Journal of Psychiatry*, vol. 182, pp. 289–290.

Hyden, L. 1997, 'Illness and narrative', *Sociology of Health and Illness*, vol. 19, pp. 48–69.

Jacoby, A. 1994, 'Felt versus enacted stigma: a concept revisited – evidence from a study of people with epilepsy in remission', *Social Science & Medicine*, vol. 38, pp. 269–274.

Jamison, K. 1998, 'Stigma and manic depression: a psychologist's experience', *The Lancet*, vol. 352, pp. 1053.

Jones, E. E., Farina, A., Hastorf, A. H., Markus, H., Miller, D. T. and Scott, R. A. 1984, *Social Stigma: The Psychology of Marked Relationships*, Freeman, New York.

Kalichman, S., Nachimson, D., Cherry, C. and Williams, E. 1998, 'AIDS treatment advances and behavioural prevention setbacks: preliminary assessment of reduced perceived threat of HIV–AIDS', *Health Psychology*, vol. 17, pp. 546–550.

Kelly, M. 1992, 'Self, identity and radical surgery', *Sociology of Health and Illness*, vol. 14, pp. 390–415.

Kelly, M. and Field, D. 1996, 'Medical sociology, chronic illness and the body', *Sociology of Health and Illness*, vol. 18, pp. 241–257.

Kelly, M. and Field, D. 1998, 'Conceptualising chronic illness', in *Sociological Perspectives on Health, Illness and Health Care*, D. Field and S. Taylor, eds., Blackwell Scientific, Oxford.

Kennedy, A., Gately, C. and Rogers, A. 2004, *Assessing the Process of Embedding EPP in the NHS: Preliminary Survey of PCT Pilot Sites*, National Primary Care Research and Development Centre, University of Manchester.

Kinniburgh, J., Scott, P., Gottlieb, M. and Power, L. 2001, *Prejudice, Discrimination and HIV*, Terrence Higgins Trust, London.

Klawiter, M. 2004, 'Breast cancer in two regimes: the impact of social movements on illness experience', *Sociology of Health and Illness*, vol. 26, pp. 845–874.

Kleinman, A. 1988, *The Illness Narratives: Suffering, Healing and the Human Conditions*, Basic Books, New York.

Klockars, C. 1974, *The Professional Fence*, Tavistock Publications, London.

Knudson-Cooper, M. 1981, 'Adjustment to visible stigma: the case of the severely burned', *Social Science & Medicine*, vol. 15B, pp. 31–44.

Kowalewski, M. 1988, 'Double stigma and boundary maintenance: how gay men deal with AIDS', *Journal of Contemporary Ethnography*, vol. 17, pp. 211–228.

La Piere, R. 1934, 'Attitudes versus actions', *Social Forces*, vol. 13, p. 230.

Laking, P. 2005, Attempts at lyrical poetry. Unpublished.

Lawton, J. 2003, 'Lay experiences of health and illness: past research and future agendas', *Sociology of Health and Illness*, vol. 25, pp. 23–40.

Lee, K., Solts, B. and Burns, J. 2002, 'Investigating the psychosocial impact of anti-HIV combination therapies', *AIDS Care*, vol. 14, no. 6, pp. 851–857.

Lee, P. 2002, 'Shooting for the moon: politics and disability at the beginning of the twenty-first century,' in *Disability Studies Today*, C. Barnes, M. Oliver and L. Barton, eds, Polity Press, Cambridge, pp. 139–161.

Leete, E. 1987, 'The treatment of schizophrenia: a patient's perspective', *Hospital and Community Psychiatry*, vol. 38, pp. 486–491.

Lichtenstein, K., Wanke, C., Henry, K., Thompson, M., Muurahainen, N. and Kotler, D. 2004, 'Estimated prevalence of HIV-associated adipose redistribution syndrome (HARS) – abnormal abdominal fat accumulation – in HIV-infected patients', *Antiviral Therapy*, vol. 9, p. L33.

Link, B. G. 1987, 'Understanding labeling effects in the area of mental disorders: an assessment of the effects of expectations of rejection', *American Sociological Review*, vol. 52, pp. 96–112.

Link, B. G. and Phelan, J. C. 1999, 'Labeling and stigma,' in *The Handbook of the Sociology of Mental Health*, C. S. Aneshensel and J. C. Phelan, eds, Plenum, New York.

Link, B. and Phelan, J. 2001, 'Conceptualizing stigma', *Annual Review of Sociology*, vol. 27, pp. 363–385.

Link, B. G., Cullen, F. T., Frank, J. and Wozniak, J. 1987, 'The social rejection of ex-mental patients: understanding why labels matter', *American Journal of Sociology*, vol. 92, pp. 1461–1500.

Link, B., Cullen, F., Struening, E., Shrout, P. and Dohrenwend, B. 1989, 'A modified labeling theory approach to mental disorders: an empirical assessment', *American Sociological Review*, vol. 54, pp. 400–423.

Link, B. G., Struening, E. L., Rahav, M., Phelan, J. C. and Nuttbrock, L. 1997, 'On stigma and its consequences: evidence from a longitudinal study of men with dual diagnoses of mental illness and substance abuse', *Journal of Health and Social Behavior*, vol. 38, pp. 177–190.

Link, B., Phelan, J., Bresnahan, M., Stueve, A. and Pescosolido, B. 1999, 'Public conceptions of mental illness: labels, causes, dangerousness, and social distance', *American Journal of Public Health*, vol. 89, pp. 1328–1333.

Lipton, F., Cohn, C., Fischer, E. and Katz, S. 1981, 'Schizophrenia: a network crisis', *Schizophrenia Bulletin*, vol. 7, pp. 144–151.

Lupton, D. 1999, *Risk*, Routledge, London.

Lupton, D. 2003, *Medicine as Culture*, 2nd edn, Sage, London.

Lyman, S. M. and Scott, M. B. 1970, *A Sociology of the Absurd*, Appleton-Century-Crofts, New York.

Lyon, D. 1999, *Postmodernity*, 2nd edn, Open University Press, Buckingham.

McCreanor, T., Moewaka Barnes, H., Gregory, M., Kaiwai, H. and Borell, S. 2005, 'Consuming identities: alcohol marketing and the commodification of youth experience', *Addiction Research and Theory*, vol. 13, no. 6, pp. 579–590.

McIntosh, J. and McKeganey, N. 2000, 'Addicts' narratives of recovery from drug use: constructing a non-addict identity', *Social Science & Medicine*, vol. 50, no. 10, pp. 1501–1510.

MacIntyre, A. 1981, *After Virtue: A Study in Moral Theory*, Duckworth, London.

Macmillan Cancer Support 2007, Working through cancer: a guide for employees. Online. Available at: www.macmillan.org.uk/Documents/Support_Material/Get_support/Working_through_cancer/Employee_booklet.pdf (accessed 15 September 2008).

Macpherson, W. 1999, *The Stephen Lawrence Inquiry: Report of an Inquiry*, The Stationery Office, London.

Mad Pride 2008, MAD PRIDE is committed to ending discrimination against psychiatric patients, promoting survivor equality and celebrating Mad culture. Online. Available at: www.ctono.freeserve.co.uk/id17.htm (accessed 20 June 2008).

Mak, W. W. S., Mo, P. K. H., Cheung, R. Y. M., Woo, J., Cheung, F. M. and Lee, D. 2006, 'Comparative stigma of HIV/AIDS, SARS, and Tuberculosis in Hong Kong', *Social Science & Medicine*, vol. 63, no. 7, pp. 1912–1922.

Mak, W. W. S., Poon, C. Y. M., Pun, L. Y. K. and Cheung, S. F. 2007, 'Meta-analysis of stigma and mental health', *Social Science & Medicine*, vol. 65, no. 2, pp. 245–261.

Markowitz, F. 1998, 'The effects of stigma on the psychological well-being and life satisfaction of persons with mental illness', *Journal of Health and Social Behavior*, vol. 39, pp. 335–347.

Markowitz, F. 2005, 'Sociological models of mental illness stigma,' in *On the Stigma of Mental Illness: Practical Strategies for Research and Social Change*, P. W. Corrigan, ed., American Psychological Association, Washington DC, pp. 129–144.

Marks, D. 1999, *Disability: Controversial Debates and Psychosocial Perspectives*, Routledge, London.

Mason, T. and Mercer, D. 1999, *A Sociology of the Mentally Disordered Offender*, Longman, London.

Mason, T., Carlisle, C., Watkins, C. and Whitehead, E. (eds) 2001, *Stigma and Social Exclusion in Healthcare*, Routledge, London.

Mathieson, C. M. and Stam, H. J. 1995, 'Renegotiating identity: cancer narratives', *Sociology of Health and Illness*, vol. 17, pp. 283–306.

Maticka-Tyndale, E., Adam, B. D. and Cohen, J. J. 2002, 'To work or not to work: combination therapies and HIV', *Qualitative Health Research*, vol. 12, no. 10, pp. 1353–1372.

Mayfield Arnold, E., Rice, E., Flannery, D. and Rotheram-Borus, M. 2008, 'HIV disclosure among adults living with HIV', *AIDS Care*, vol. 20, no. 1, pp. 80–92.

Measham, F. and Brain, K. 2005, ' "Binge" drinking, British alcohol policy and the new culture of intoxication', *Crime Media Culture*, vol. 1, no. 3, pp. 262–283.

Mental Health Alliance 2007, Mental Health Bill remains a missed opportunity for humane and progressive legislation. Online. Available at: www.mentalhealthalliance.org.uk/news/prendofbill.html (accessed 3 July 2007).

Mills, C. 1940, 'Situated actions and vocabularies of motive', *American Sociological Review*, vol. 5, pp. 904–913.

Mind 2001, Latest Mind survey provides good news. Online. Available at: www.mind.org.uk/News+policy+and+campaigns/Press+archive/Latest+Mind+survey+provides+good+news.htm (accessed 6 August 2008).

Mind 2008, Charity appalled as new survey reveals the extent of the damage still being caused by ECT. Online. Available at: www.mind.org.uk/News+policy+and+campaigns/Press+archive/Charity+appalled+as+new+survey+reveals+the+extent+of+the+damage+still+being+caused+by+ECT.htm (accessed 19 June 2008).

Moatti, J. P. and Souteyrand, Y. 2000, 'HIV/AIDS social and behavioural research: past advances and thoughts about the future', *Social Science & Medicine*, vol. 50, no. 11, pp. 1519–1532.

Moore, O. 1996, *Looking AIDS in the Face*, Pan Macmillan, London.

Moorhead, J. 2008, 'Coming to their senses', *The Guardian* 29 April 2008.

Morris, J. 1991, *Pride Against Prejudice: Transforming Attitudes to Disability*, Women's Press, London.

National AIDS Trust 2007, *From a Positive Perspective: Key Issues for People Living with HIV in the UK*, National AIDS Trust, London.

National AIDS Trust 2008, *Public Attitudes towards HIV 2007*, National AIDS Trust, London.

Navon, L. 1996, 'Beyond constructionism and pessimism: theoretical implications of leprosy destigmatisation campaigns in Thailand', *Social Science & Medicine*, vol. 18, no. 2, pp. 258–276.

Nunnally, J. 1961, *Popular Conceptions of Mental Health: Their Development and Change*, Holt, Rinehart and Winston, New York.

O'Connor, C. 2005, Scott bites back. Online. Available at: www.positivenation.co.uk/issue118/features/feature1/feature1.htm (accessed 5 August 2008).

Office of National Statistics 2008, Census. Online. Available at: www.ons.gov.uk/census/index.html (accessed 3 July 2008).

Oliver, M. 1990, *The Politics of Disablement*, Macmillan, Basingstoke.

Oliver, M. 1996a, *Understanding Disability: From Theory to Practice*, Macmillan, Basingstoke.

Oliver, M. 1996b, 'A sociology of disability or a disablist sociology?,' in *Disability and Society: Emerging Issues and Insights*, L. Barton, ed., Longman, London, pp. 18–42.

Page, R. M. 1984, *Stigma*, Routledge & Keegan Paul, London.

Palella, F. J., Delaney, K. M., Moorman, A. C., Loveless, M. O., Fuhrer, J., Satten, G. A., Aschman, D. J. and Holmberg, S. D. 1998, 'Declining morbidity and mortality among patients with advanced human immunodeficiency virus infection. HIV Outpatient Study Investigators', *New England Journal of Medicine*, vol. 338, no. 13, pp. 853–860.

Parker, H. 2005, 'Normalization as a barometer: recreational drug use and the consumption of leisure by younger Britons', *Addiction Research and Theory*, vol. 13, no. 3, pp. 205–215.

Parker, H., Bakx, K. and Newcombe, R. 1988, *Living with Heroin*, Open University Press, Milton Keynes.

Parker, H., Measham, F. and Aldridge, J. 1995, *Drugs Futures: Changing Patterns of Drug Use Amongst English Youth*, Institute for the Study of Drug Dependence, London.

Parker, R. and Aggleton, P. 2003, 'HIV and AIDS-related stigma and discrimination: a conceptual framework and implications for action', *Social Science & Medicine*, vol. 57, pp. 13–24.

Partridge, J. 2006, 'From burns unit to boardroom', *British Medical Journal*, vol. 332, pp. 956–959.

Pausch, R. 2007, The last lecture: really achieving your childhood dreams. Online. Available at: www.youtube.com/watch?v=ji5_MqicxSo (accessed 26 July 2008).

Pausch, R. and Zaslow, J. 2008, *The Last Lecture*, Hodder & Stoughton, London.

Paykel, E., Tylee, A., Wright, A., Priest, R., Rix, S. and Hart, D. 1997, 'The Defeat Depression campaign: psychiatry in the public arena', *American Journal of Psychiatry*, vol. 154, pp. 59–65.

Perkins, R. and Repper, J. 2001, 'Exclusive language?,' in *Stigma and Social Inclusion in Healthcare*, T. Mason, C. Carlisle, C. Watkins and E. Whitehead, eds, Routledge, London, pp. 147–157.

Persson, A. 2003, 'Shaping lives: psychosocial effects of lipodystrophy', *HIV Australia*, vol. 2, pp. 14–15.

Persson, A. 2004, 'Incorporating *Pharmakon*: HIV, medicine, and body shape change', *Body and Society*, vol. 4, pp. 45–67.

Persson, A. and Newman, C. 2006, 'Potency and vulnerability: troubled "selves" in the context of antiretroviral therapy', *Social Science & Medicine*, vol. 63, pp. 1586–1596.

Persson, A., Race, K. and Wakeford, E. 2003, 'HIV health in context: negotiating medical technology and lived experience', *Health*, vol. 7, no. 4, pp. 397–415.

Pescosolido, B. A., Martin, J. K., Lang, A. and Olafsdottir, S. 2008, 'Rethinking theoretical approaches to stigma: a framework integrating normative influences on stigma (FINIS)', *Social Science & Medicine*, vol. 67, no. 3, pp. 431–440.

Petrak, J. A., Doyle, A. M., Smith, A., Skinner, C. and Hedge, B. 2001, 'Factors associated with self-disclosure of HIV serostatus to significant others', *British Journal of Health Psychology*, vol. 6, pp. 69–79.

Petros, G., Airhihenbuwa, C., Simbayi, L., Ramlagan, S. and Brown, B. 2006, 'HIV/ AIDS and "othering" in South Africa: the blame goes on', *Culture, Health and Sexuality.*, vol. 8, no. 1, pp. 67–77.

Phelan, J. C. and Link, B.G. 1998, 'The growing belief that people with mental illness are violent: the role of the dangerousness criterion for civil commitment', *Social Pyschiatry and Psychiatric Epidemiology*, vol. 33, supplement 1, pp. S7–S12.

Phelan, J., Link, B., Stueve, A. and Pescosolido, B. 2000, 'Public conceptions of mental illness in 1950 and 1996: what is mental illness and is it to be feared?', *Journal of Health and Social Behavior*, vol. 41, pp. 188–207.

Phelan, J. C., Link, B. G. and Dovidio, J. F. 2008, 'Stigma and prejudice: one animal or two?', *Social Science & Medicine*, vol. 67, no. 3, pp. 358–367.

Philo, G., Secker, J., Platt, S., Henderson, L., McLaughlin, G. and Burnside, J. 1994, 'The impact of the mass media on public images of mental illness: media content and audience belief', *Health Education Journal*, vol. 53, pp. 271–281.

Pierret, J. 2003, 'The illness experience: state of knowledge and perspectives for research', *Sociology of Health and Illness*, vol. 25, pp. 4–22.

Pilgrim, D. and Rogers, A. E. 2005, 'Psychiatrists as social engineers: a study of an anti-stigma campaign', *Social Science & Medicine*, vol. 61, no. 12, pp. 2546–2556.

Plummer, K. 1997, *Telling Sexual Stories: Power Change and Social Worlds*, 2nd edn, Routledge, London and New York.

Plummer, K. 2008, 'The moral career of the transplant patient: personal experiences and sociological reflections', seminar at the University of Essex, 4 February.

Plumridge, E. and Chetwynd, J. 1998, 'The moral universe of injecting drug users in the era of AIDS: sharing injecting equipment and the protection of moral standing', *AIDS Care*, vol. 10, no. 6, pp. 723–733.

Pound, P., Gompertz, P. and Ebrahim, S. 1998, 'Illness in the context of older age: the case of stroke', *Sociology of Health and Illness*, vol. 20, pp. 489–506.

Power, R., Tate, H. L., McGill, S. M. and Taylor, C. 2003, 'A qualitative study of the psychosocial implications of lipodystrophy syndrome on HIV positive individuals', *Sexually Transmitted Infections*, vol. 79, no. 2, pp. 137–141.

Radley, A. (ed.) 1993a, *World of Illness: Biographical and Cultural Perspectives on Health and Disease*, Routledge, London.

Radley, A. 1993b, 'The role of metaphor in adjustment to chronic illness,' in *World of Illness: Biographical and Cultural Perspectives on Health and Disease*, A. Radley, ed., Routledge, London, pp. 109–123.

Radley, A. and Billig, M. 1996, 'Accounts of health and illness: dilemmas and representations', *Sociology of Health and Illness*, vol. 18, no. 2, pp. 220–240.

Rahav, M., Struening, E. and Andrews, H. 1984, 'Opinions on mental illness in Israel', *Social Science & Medicine*, vol. 19, pp. 1151–1158.

Rasinski, K., Woll, P. and Cooke, A. 2005, 'Stigma and substance use disorders,' in *On the Stigma of Mental Illness: Practical Strategies for Research and Social Change*, P. Corrigan, ed., American Psychological Association, Washington DC, pp. 219–236.

Read, J. and Baker, S. 1996, *Not Just Sticks and Stones: A Survey of Stigma, Taboos and Discrimination Experienced by People with Mental Health Problems*, Mind, London.

Reed Committe 1992, *Review of Mental Health and Social Services for Mentally Disordered Offenders and Others Requiring Similar Services*, The Stationery Office, London.

Reidpath, D., Chan, K., Gifford, S. and Allotey, P. 2005, ' "He hath the French pox": stigma, social value and social exclusion', *Sociology of Health and Illness*, vol. 27, no. 4, pp. 468–489.

Riessman, C. 1990, 'Strategic uses of narrative in the presentation of self and illness: a research note', *Social Science & Medicine*, vol. 30, no. 11, pp. 1195–2000.

Rigg, J. 2007, 'Disabling attitudes? Public perspectives on disabled people', in *British Social Attitudes: The 23rd Report – Perspectives on a Changing Society*, Sage, London.

Robinson, I. 1990, 'Personal narratives, social careers and medical courses: analysing life trajectories in autobiographies of people with multiple sclerosis', *Social Science & Medicine*, vol. 30, pp. 1173–1186.

Rogers, A., Pilgrim, D. and Lacey, R. 1993, *Experiencing Psychiatry: Users' Views of Services*, Macmillan, Basingstoke.

Room, R. 2005, 'Stigma, social inequality and alcohol and drug use', *Drug and Alcohol Review*, vol. 24, no. 2, pp. 143–155.

Rosenfield, S. 1997, 'Labeling mental illness: the effects of services and perceived stigma life satisfaction', *American Sociological Review*, vol. 62, pp. 660–672.

Rosengarten, M., Imrie, J., Flowers, P., Davis, M. and Hart, G. J. 2004, 'After the euphoria: HIV medical technologies from the perspective of their prescribers', *Sociology of Health and Illness*, vol. 26, no. 5, pp. 575–595.

Royal College of Psychiatrists (2003) Drugs and alcohol – whose problem is it anyway? Online. Available at: www.rcpsych.ac.uk/campaigns/changingminds/mentaldisorders/alcoholanddrugmisuse.aspx (accessed 18 April 2008).

Ryan, T. 1998, 'Perceived risks associated with mental illness: beyond homicide and suicide', *Social Science & Medicine*, vol. 46, no. 2, pp. 287–297.

Rymes, B. 1995, 'The construction of moral agency in the narratives of high-school drop-outs', *Discourse and Society*, vol. 6, no. 4, pp. 495–516.

Sanders, C., Donovan, J. and Dieppe, P. 2002, 'The significance and consequences of having painful and disabled joints in older age: co-existing accounts of normal and disrupted biographies', *Sociology of Health and Illness*, vol. 24, pp. 227–253.

Sandstrom, K. 1990, 'Confronting deadly disease: the drama of identity construction among gay men with AIDS', *Journal of Contemporary Ethnography*, vol. 19, pp. 271–294.

Sartorius, N. 1998, 'Stigma: what can psychiatrists do about it?', *Lancet*, vol. 352, pp. 1058–1059.

Saunders, D. S. and Burgoyne, R. W. 2002, 'Evaluating health-related wellbeing outcomes among outpatient adults with human immunodeficiency virus infection in the HAART era', *International Journal of STD and AIDS*, vol. 13, no. 10, pp. 683–690.

Sayce, L. 1998, 'Stigma, discrimination and social exclusion: what's in a word?', *Journal of Mental Health*, vol. 7, no. 4, pp. 331–343.

Sayce, L. 2000, *From Psychiatric Patient to Citizen: Overcoming Discrimination and Social Exclusion*, Macmillan Press, Basingstoke and London.

Scambler, G. 2004, 'Re-framing stigma: felt and enacted stigma and challenges to the sociology of chronic and disabling conditions', *Social Theory and Health*, vol. 2, pp. 29–46.

Scambler, G. and Hopkins, A. 1986, 'Being epileptic: coming to terms with stigma', *Sociology of Health and Illness*, vol. 8, pp. 26–43.

Scheff, T. 1966, *Being Mentally Ill: A Sociology Theory*, Aldine, Chicago.

Scheid, T. 2005, 'Stigma as a barrier to employment: mental disability and the Americans with Disabilities Act', *International Journal of Law and Psychiatry*, vol. 28, no. 6, pp. 670–690.

Schneider, J. and Conrad, P. 1981, 'Medical and social typologies: the case of epilepsy', *Social Science & Medicine*, vol. 15A, pp. 211–219.

Schulze, B. and Angermeyer, M. C. 2003, 'Subjective experiences of stigma: a focus group study of schizophrenic patients, their relatives and mental health professionals', *Social Science & Medicine*, vol. 56, no. 2, pp. 299–312.

Shakespeare, T. 2008, Tell me another: continuing fascination with visible oddity betrays the overall lack of progress in the way British television continues to represent minorities. Online. Available at: www.equalityhumanrights.com/en/newsandcomment/speakerscorner/Pages/Tellmeanother_TomShakespeare.aspx (accessed 30 January 2008).

Shakespeare, T. and Watson, N. 2001, 'Disability, politics and recognition,' in *Handbook of Disability Studies*, G. L. Albrecht, K. Seelman and M. Bury, eds, Sage, Thousand Oaks, California, pp. 546–564.

Shaughnessy, P. 2001, 'Not in my back yard: stigma from a personal perspective,' in *Stigma and Social Exclusion in Health Care*, T. Mason, C. Carlisle, C. Watkins and E. Whitehead, eds., Routledge, London, pp. 181–189.

Shepherd, A. 1966, 'One mind,' in *Stigma: The Experience of Disability*, P. Hunt, ed., Geoffrey Chapman, London, pp. 54–67.

Sherr, L., Sherr, A. H. and Orchard, S. 1998, 'Discrimination and HIV', *Journal of the American Medical Association*, vol. 279, no. 11, p. 834.

SHiFT 2007, Action on stigma: employers' views on promoting mental health and ending discrimination at work. Online. Available at: www.shift.org.uk (accessed 27 June 2008).

Shilling, C. 1993, *The Body and Social Theory*, Sage, London.

Siegel, K. and Lekas, H.-M. 2002, 'AIDS as a chronic illness: psychosocial implications', *AIDS*, vol. 16, Supplement 4, pp. S69–S76.

Sontag, S. 1991, *Illness as Metaphor and AIDS and its Metaphors*, Penguin, London.

South, N. 1999, 'Debating drugs and everyday life: normalisation, prohibition and "otherness"', in *Drugs: Cultures, Controls and Everyday Life*, N. South, ed., Sage, London, pp. 1–16.

South, N., Smith, R. and Green, G. 2005, 'Mental health, social order, system disorder', *Criminal Justice Matters*, vol. 61, pp. 4–5.

Sowell, R. L., Phillips, K. D. and Grier, J. 1998, 'Restructuring life to face the future: the perspective of men after a positive response to protease inhibitor therapy', *AIDS Patient Care and STDs*, vol. 12, no. 1, pp. 33–42.

Stanley, L. D. 2003, 'Transforming AIDS: the moral management of stigmatized identity', *Anthropology and Medicine*, vol. 6, no. 1, pp. 103–120.

Strauss, A. and Glaser, B. 1975, *Chronic Illness and the Quality of Life*, Mosby, St Louis.

Stuber, J., Meyer, I. and Link, B. 2008, 'Stigma, prejudice, discrimination and health', *Social Science & Medicine*, vol. 67, no. 3, pp. 351–357.

Sudbury, A. 2008, Baldy's Blog. Online. Available at: http://baldyblog.freshblogs.co.uk/ (accessed 20 June 2008).

Sumner, C. 1994, *The Sociology of Deviance: An Obituary*, Open University Press, Buckingham.

Sunday Times 2007, 'Deaf demand right to designer deaf child', 23 December. Online. Available at: www.timesonline.co.uk/tol/news/uk/health/article3087367.ece (accessed 6 August 2008).

Sykes, G. and Matza, D. 1957, 'Techniques of neutralization: a theory of delinquency', *American Sociological Review*, vol. 22, pp. 664–670.

Szasz, T. 1974, *The Myth of Mental Illness: Foundations of a Theory of Personal Conduct*, Harper & Row, New York.

Takahashi, L. M., Wiebe, D. and Rodriguez, R. 2001, 'Navigating the time–space context of HIV and AIDS: daily routines and access to care', *Social Science & Medicine*, vol. 53, no. 7, pp. 845–863.

Taylor, D. and Bury, M. 2007, 'Chronic illness, expert patients and care transition', *Sociology of Health and Illness*, vol. 29, no. 1, pp. 27–45.

Thomas, C. 2007, *Sociologies of Disability and Illness: Contested Ideas in Disability Studies and Medical Sociology*, Palgrave Macmillan, Basingstoke.

Thompson, B. 2003, 'Lazarus phenomena: an exploratory study of gay men living with HIV', *Social Work in Health Care*, vol. 37, no. 1, pp. 87–114.

UNAIDS 2008, HIV-related travel restrictions. Online. Available at: www.unaids. org/en/KnowledgeCentre/Resources/FeatureStories/archive/2008/20080304 (accessed 11 September 2008).

UNAIDS/WHO 2007, *AIDS Epidemic Update*, UNAIDS and World Health Organization, Geneva.

UPIAS 1976, *Fundamental Principles of Disability*, Union of the Physically Impaired Against Segregation, London.

Valantin, M., Aubron-Olivier, C., Ghosn, J., Laglenne, E., Pauchard, M., Schoen, H., Bousquet, R., Katz, P., Costagliola, D. and Katlama, C. 2003, 'Polylactic acid implants (New-Fill) to correct facial lipoatrophy in HIV-infected patients: results of the open-label study VEGA', *AIDS*, vol. 17, pp. 2533–2535.

Ville, I., Ravaud, J., Diard, C. and Paicheler, H. 1994, 'Self-representations and physical impairment: a social constructionist approach', *Sociology of Health and Illness*, vol. 16, pp. 301–321.

Wahl, O. 1999, 'Mental health consumers' experience of stigma', *Schizophrenia Bulletin*, vol. 25, no. 3, pp. 467–478.

Walk the Walk 2008, Walk the walk: uniting against breast cancer. Online. Available at: www.walkthewalk.org/Home (accessed 31 July 2008).

Warde, A. 1994, 'Consumption, identity-formation and uncertainty', *Sociology*, vol. 28, pp. 877–898.

Watson, A. and Corrigan, P. 2005, 'Challenging public stigma: a targeted approach,' in *On the Stigma of Mental Illness: Practical Strategies for Research and Social Change*, P. Corrigan, ed., American Psychological Association, Washington DC, pp. 281–295.

Weait, M. and Azad, Y. 2005, 'The criminalization of HIV transmission in England and Wales: questions of law and policy', *HIV AIDS Policy Law Review*, vol. 10, pp. 5–12.

Weatherburn, P., Ssanyu-Sseruma, W., Hickson, F., McLean, S. and Reid, D. 2003, *Project Nasah: An Investigation into the HIV Treatment Information and Other Needs of African People with HIV Resident in England*, Sigma Research, London.

Williams, G. 1984, 'The genesis of chronic illness: narrative reconstruction', *Sociology of Health and Illness*, vol. 6, pp. 175–200.

Williams, S. 1987, 'Goffman, interactionism, and the management of stigma in everyday life,' in *Sociological theory and medical sociology*, G. Scambler, ed., Tavistock Publications, London, pp. 136–164.

Williams, S. J. 2000, 'Chronic illness as biographical disruption or biographical disruption as chronic illness? Reflections on a core concept', *Sociology of Health and Illness*, vol. 22, pp. 40–67.

Williams, S. J. and Bury, M. 1989, 'Impairment, disability and handicap in chronic respiratory illness', *Social Science & Medicine*, vol. 29, pp. 609–616.

Wolff, G. 1997, 'Attitudes of the media and the public,' in *Care in the Community: Illusion or Reality?*, J. Leff, ed., John Wiley & Sons, Chichester, pp. 145–163.

Young, J. 1999, *The Exclusive Society: Social Exclusion, Crime and Difference*, Sage Publications, London.

Zhou, Y. R. 2007, ' "If you get AIDS . . . you have to endure it alone": understanding the social constructions of HIV/AIDS in China', *Social Science & Medicine*, vol. 65, no. 2, pp. 284–295.

Zola, I. 1982, *Missing Pieces: A Chronicle of Living with a Disability*, Temple University Press, Philadelphia.

Zola, I. 1993, 'Self, identity and the naming question: reflections on the language of disability', *Social Science & Medicine*, vol. 36, no. 2, pp. 167–173.

Index

blame: blameworthy behaviour 77;
double deviance of HIV and 55–6
Blaxter, M. 43, 45, 46
body: body shape 61–2; impaired body
6, 25, 42; role of technology in
fashioning 33, 35–6; self and 34–5,
44, 91
Borderline Personality Disorder 82
Born to be Different (Channel 4 TV)
116
boundaries 4, 21, 22, 23, 35, 37, 55, 78
Bradby, Hannah x
Brashers, D.E. *et al.* 59, 61, 63
British Deaf Association 117
British HIV Association x, 126n2
Brockington, I. *et al.* 93, 94
Bromley, C. *et al.* 77
Brown, H. 6
Brown, P. and Zavestoski, S. 49, 52
Brown, P. *et al.* 48, 49, 50
Bury, M. 8, 24, 37, 38, 40, 41, 42, 46
Byrne, P. 93

C: Because Cowards Get Cancer Too
(Diamond, J.) 4
Cameron, R. 119
Camp, D.L., Finlay, W.M.L. and Lyons,
E. 99
Campbell, P. 101
Carricaburu, D. and Pierret, J. 40, 43,
91
CASL (Campaign for the Abolition of
the Schizophrenia Label) 110–11
Castells, Manuel 30
Castle, S. 56
Catalan, J., Green, L. and Thorley, F. 62
Catalan, J., Meadows, J. and Douzenis,
A. 63
celebrities, and substance misuse 90
Charlton, J. 47–8
Charmaz, K. 40
Child Welfare League of America 89
Chinouya, M. and Davidson, O. 63, 67
chronic illness, definition of 7–8
City Press 66
Closer 90
Cohen, J. and Struening, E. 94
Cohen, S. 78
communism 2
community level production of stigma
22–3
concealability 15–16, 71
conceptualization of stigma 13–14
Conrad, P. 40

consciousness-raising 47, 53, 119
consumerism 33, 34, 35
contagion by HIV, symbolic
contamination and 56–7
contextual nature of stigma 112–13
controllability 16, 126n8
Corrigan, P. 14, 32, 125n5
Corrigan, P. and Cooper, A. 95
Corrigan, P. and Kleinlein, P. 17, 19
Corrigan, P. and Penn, D. 102
Corrigan, P. and Watson, A. 17, 99
Corrigan, P.W. *et al.* 93, 94, 102, 127n3
Crandall, C. and Moriarty, D. 55
Crawford, R. 21, 35, 55, 69
Creegan, Denis 6
Crisp, A. 103
Crisp, A. *et al.* 94
Crocker, J. and Major, B. 99
Crocker, J. *et al.* 16, 17
Crocker, J., Major, B. and Steele, C. 14
Crossley, N. 100, 101, 102, 109
Crossley, M.L. 40, 41, 45, 48, 50, 70
cultural change, stigma of long-term
conditions and 1–4, 9

Daily Mail 70
'dangerous individuals' 12, 73,
77–9, 79–84, 84–5; self-confessed
'dangerous individual', alternative
discourse of 84–5
dangerousness 21, 57, 75–9, 94–5, 107
Davis, K.K., Davis, J.S. and Dowler, L.
4
Davis, M. *et al.* 19, 59, 60, 63
Davison, Charlie x–xi
Davison, Hilary x
De Jong, W. 55
definitional confusion 13–15, 113–14
Del Vecchio Good, M. *et al.* 45
Demant, J. and Jarvinen, M. 90
Deng, R. *et al.* 56
'deviance': demise of 113; disavowal of
85–7; drugs and 75–6; oppression,
'deviance' and 24–6; oppression and
24–6
diagnostic advances 114
Diamond, John 4, 40–1, 45
dimensions of stigma 15–16
disability and long-term conditions,
definition of 7–8
Disability Discrimination Act (1995) 3,
9, 52, 63, 66, 107, 126n6
Disability Rights Commission 38, 52,
108

eBooks – at www.eBookstore.tandf.co.uk

A library at your fingertips!

eBooks are electronic versions of printed books. You can store them on your PC/laptop or browse them online.

They have advantages for anyone needing rapid access to a wide variety of published, copyright information.

eBooks can help your research by enabling you to bookmark chapters, annotate text and use instant searches to find specific words or phrases. Several eBook files would fit on even a small laptop or PDA.

NEW: Save money by eSubscribing: cheap, online access to any eBook for as long as you need it.

Annual subscription packages

We now offer special low-cost bulk subscriptions to packages of eBooks in certain subject areas. These are available to libraries or to individuals.

For more information please contact webmaster.ebooks@tandf.co.uk

We're continually developing the eBook concept, so keep up to date by visiting the website.

www.eBookstore.tandf.co.uk

You might also be interested in Routledge's exciting series:
Critical Studies in Health and Society

Series Editors
Simon J. Williams and Gillian Bendelow

This major new international book series takes a critical look at health in a
rapidly changing social world. The series includes theoretically sophisticated
and empirically informed contributions on cutting-edge issues from leading
figures within the sociology of health and allied disciplines and domains.
New and forthcoming titles in the series include:

Emotional Labour in Health Care: The Unmanaged Heart of Nursing
Catherine Theodosius
2008
ISBN (Hardback): 978-0-415-40953-7
ISBN (Paperback): 978-0-415-40954-4
ISBN (e-book): 978-0-203-89495-8

**Globalisation, Markets and Healthcare Policy: Redrawing the Patient as
Consumer**
Jonathan Tritter, Meri Koivusalo and Eeva Ollila
2009
ISBN (Hardback): 978-0-415-41702-0

**Medical Sociology and Old Age: Towards a Sociology of Health in Later
Life**
Paul Higgs and Ian Rees Jones
2009
ISBN (Hardback): 978-0-415-39855-8
ISBN (Paperback): 978-0-415-39860-2
ISBN (e-book): 978-0-203-88872-8